THE BLUE SUIT

Richard Rayner

THE BLUE SUIT

PICADOR

First published 1995 by Picador

an imprint of Macmillan General Books
Cavaye Place London SW10 9PG
and Basingstoke

Associated companies throughout the world

ISBN 0 330 33821 8

The author and publishers gratefully acknowledge Faber and Faber Ltd
for permission to reproduce an extract from 'Burnt Norton'
from *The Collected Poems 1909–1962* by T. S. Eliot

A CIP catalogue record for this book is available from
the British Library

Typeset by CentraCet Limited, Cambridge
Printed by Mackays of Chatham plc, Kent

For Paivi

THE BLUE SUIT

One

What began it all was an offhand remark, so uncannily acute I had to laugh. I shouldn't have been surprised, since Paivi, my girlfriend and wife soon-to-be, has the best emotional radar of anyone I've ever met. Even so, this one-liner released a story, which led to others – one confession veiling the next. Perhaps we all have this dream, to tell everything and yet not forfeit love – the only sinner not to be roasted. We dream of redemption, of being better, not richer, but more compassionate, human. In my late thirties Paivi made me see I'd buried my own coming of age.

It was the end of April 1992, the second day of the Los Angeles riots, and I was watching at a time when I'd lost my way. My father had died and I couldn't put that behind me. I'd left London telling my previous girlfriend I was stepping out for a pint of milk. I'd behaved with breath-taking carelessness towards my friends, my family, and now, nine months later, with cash running out, I felt as though I was beating my head against the wall; once I actually did beat my head against the wall and Paivi had to rush me to the hospital with a concussion. This was only partly comical. I'd spent three years working on a book and the thing wasn't finished. I wasn't a writer, I was Walter Mitty, and sometimes it felt like the only things between me and twenty thousand feet of thin air were the *ta-pocketa-pocketa-pocketa* of a Remington typewriter and my many bookcases stuffed with first editions: Byron, the three-volume life by Leslie Marchand; the *Collected Poems* of Frank O'Hara; Raymond Chandler's *The Big Sleep*; *A Handful of Dust* by Evelyn Waugh, and so on and on. I'm obsessed with books, and I'd accumulated more than three thousand since we'd been here, to add to the eight thousand back in London, and the mere thousand in Yorkshire, where I was born. When I escaped into a second-hand bookshop that felt like coming home. I went into a trance.

So there Paivi and I were, outside the 7-Eleven on La Brea. A white middle-class couple, about our age, dressed in identical white nylon jogging suits, emerged from the store carrying boxes filled with soup cans, toilet rolls and kitchen towels. Probably the more expensive items, the liquor and so on, had gone by then. They'd grabbed what they could to load into their Volvo.

'This is extraordinary,' I said. 'They don't need the stuff. They're not so different from us. We don't even own jogging suits and *we're* not looting.'

Paivi lowered her Ray-Bans and peeped over them like Lolita. 'Yes, Richard,' she said. 'But what if the store were filled with Nabokov first editions?'

Two

A screen rolled down, the lights went off, the titles came up, and all the boys, we were only boys, settled in hard wooden chairs to watch. *Greyfriars Bobby* was set in Edinburgh and told the story of a little terrier whose master died, a little terrier named Greyfriars Bobby. Greyfriars Bobby sat on his master's grave and pined. He refused to budge. He refused to eat or drink. After fifteen minutes I heard a snuffle or two around me, and I was having to swallow hard myself when an old lady offered bones to Greyfriars Bobby, and choice steak, but still he turned his little head away. He had to be loyal to his master even though he was beginning to get poorly himself and the boy next to me couldn't stand it any more. He broke down and started to sob, mouth gaping, spit dribbling down his chin. Things looked bad now for poor Greyfriars Bobby, it looked like he was going to die, and soon everyone was joining in, me as well, the entire first two years of the school, sixty small boys wailing, blubbing away their homesickness.

I was nine. The boarding school my father had found

wasn't far from Llandudno in North Wales, where my sister, my brother, and I had been living with him after my mother left, but it was a whole other world, a white Victorian building with turrets and battlements, approached up a hill. Staff members were either old and eccentric, monsters even, in tweed jackets, or young and eager, whistling as they strode about, sucking on pipes and mindful of their dreams. Lavatories had no doors. Windows iced up in winter when even scalding radiators didn't keep the classrooms warm. Dormitories had no heating at all and offences, such as talking after lights out, were punished by beatings with a split cane in Room 100. But the peak of my dread came on Sunday mornings when we were required to sit down and write a letter to our parents. I couldn't write to my father, since he came to see me every week, so I wrote to my mother, and there was one particular master – bald, eyes full of an anger I didn't understand – who, when all the letters had been collected, called me to the front of the class and asked . . . Mrs M. Michie? Didn't I have any parents of my own to write to? I tried in a whisper to explain that Mrs M. Michie was my mother, that she'd married again, but he always interrupted, 'This boy doesn't even *know his own name.*' And then he invited the other boys to laugh; they duly obliged.

Stairs and corridors were covered with highly polished linoleum which squeaked as your sandals slid across it. You could hear someone coming fifty yards away. At the end of every corridor there was a tweed jacket, ready and waiting if you should dare to run. Room 100. Running was forbidden, except on the playing fields, where we swarmed about in mud, beehives of boys pursuing one single soccer or rugby ball. Soggy puddings were a part of the routine, as were 'magic circles', each boy masturbating the one to his right. Aged eleven, when I won the Thomas B. Costain English composition prize I was given, by mistake, *Lord of the Rings*, when I'd asked for *Lord of the Flies*. I don't think a joke was intended.

I started to suffer from migraines, stroboscopic shimmerings at the edges of my vision, light shaken into its constituent colours. I had a dreamy sensation that the world was being snipped away. This was followed by two hours of blinding headache, then vomiting until bile came retching out of the liver. The first time this happened I was assumed to be putting it on, but the attacks became so frequent that I was allowed to sit them out in a darkened room, and then I was able to fake one, from time to time, picking the moment, rocking my head so it was the master who noticed my simulated moon-faced vacancy, the first true sign of migraine.

I went there in 1966 and stayed three years. Each day a growing gang gathered in the fifth-form classroom, singing along as Radio 1 played its record of the week, 'make it better *better* BETTER, *oooow*-WAAAAGH . . . na, na-na, na-na-na-na, na-na-na-na, HEY JUDE.' One morning I got to do the solo: 'Hey Judie, Judiejudiejudie, *neeeooooow* WAH.'

It was the summer men walked on the moon. One

Sunday my brother Keith, not my father, was waiting when I trooped out of chapel.

'Something's happened to Dad,' he said.

My father's clothes had been found on the beach at Deganwy. He was missing, presumed drowned.

My stepfather bought the Old Manor, a sandstone house near Bradford back in Yorkshire. Oliver Cromwell had slept there, the story went, two nights before the Battle of Marston Moor. So it was yet another move. The door from the dining room to the kitchen passageway was so low only my mother could sail under without risking concussion. Aged twelve I was barely five feet four, but still unable to make it through. My time there featured bruised foreheads and insomniac nights, through which I read until dawn: P. G. Wodehouse, *Wuthering Heights*, *Pride and Prejudice*. For several weeks I strutted about, flicking my cuffs and pulling up an imaginary pair of polished boots, pretending to be Darcy.

I went, first to a local grammar, and then two years later, to a boarding school back in North Wales, another town by the sea, this time Colwyn Bay – which had none of the grace and frolic of Llandudno. There was a local boy, Richard Evans, whose father owned the Hi-Hat Ice Cream Company in Conwy, across the estuary from where we'd lived. Richard Evans was tall, with glistening round cheeks and long fair hair – Shelley in a pair of National Health specs, though his tastes ran more to the modern. When pimples appeared on my chin and forehead he addressed me as the young man carbuncular. He asked if those were the corpses I'd planted at Mylae, starting to sprout. '*Mon semblable, mon frère!*' he cried. We were alone in the library one afternoon. Rain rattled against the windows. He made a show of putting away a volume of the *Encyclopaedia Britannica*, sliding it back so the set was complete. 'I've been looking up homosexuality,' he said. 'They say that if you have no father you're probably going to turn out to be one. A homosexual. A *queer*.'

At this time, at this particular third-rate British public school, homosexuality was the worst imaginable fate. Everyone was obsessed with not being queer. If you were bad at games, you were a queer. Good in class? *Definitely* queer. Really rotten in class? Probably queer as well. Not shaving yet, wanking too often, not wanking at all, wanting the door shut when you took a shit? Queer.

I stood there tingling while Richard Evans said that he'd seen a newspaper story about the disappearance of a local businessman. 'The headline was WHERE IS JACK RAYNER? It said that lots of money was missing as well. Is that your dad?'

Rain drummed at the panes, streaming down. I knew I should stick up for my father, and myself. I knew what I should say, something like – Yes, that's him, I don't know if he's dead or alive. He's probably a crook. I hear he managed to sell fifty odd cars without paying for them. So what?

'No,' I said. 'That's not my dad. Must be someone else. Definitely not him.'

'I heard you'd lived in Llandudno.'

'I think I went there once,' I said. It's just down the road, isn't it?'

Richard Evans never mentioned this again.

I grew my hair. I was a small boy with a fast tongue, shy prickliness mistaken for wilful rebellion by the school staff. This, together with an ability to tell jokes and reel off Monty Python sketches, won me a place in the crowd. I played air guitar to Cream and Led Zeppelin, scoffed at queers, and gobbed off the end of the pier into the dirty brown heave of the Irish Sea. Sundays I put on my best blazer, walked to the Forte's Splendido Café and raised a milkshake in hopeful, hopeless toast to Sue Barrand, a blonde from the local girls' school.

It was a Thursday, it was in May, and the first book I stole was *Dracula*, with its sexy air of blood and danger. Christopher Lee was on the paperback cover. It was in a small newsagent's shop, not far from school. Once the book was off the spinner I flipped through a few pages, thrilled and afraid, then ducked down towards the soft-drinks shelf and tucked it inside my blazer. The second was Nik Cohn's *Awopbopaloobopalapbamboom*, the Paladin edition, a lovely thing with the Guy Peeleart illustration of Elvis. I was fourteen and the kick I felt, the delight in those books, was no doubt increased by the fact of their illicit acquisition, though at the time I was just as happy buying books or borrowing from the library. I wallowed in Agatha Christie, Wodehouse, and Evelyn Waugh, each answering, as they differently did, a need for excitement on the page. Dismayed by Emily Brontë's low output, I read *Wuthering Heights* perhaps eighteen times, until at last I didn't have to follow the sentences at all: the mere glimpse of a passage's printed appearance would recall that first excitment. I picked up Hemingway, Camus, Dostoevsky, more Jane Austen, the skinhead books by Richard Allen, *A Clockwork Orange* and two or three others by Anthony Burgess – the usual crowd, none of whom I imagined were connected with the *English litera-ture* I was made to study. I read *The Great Gatsby* in Penguin Modern Classics, astonished that a book could reach inside with so delicate a hand. I was so puzzled when *Wuthering Heights* turned up on the A-level syllabus I assumed it must be a mistake, or another book with the same title. I expected someone to pop up and snatch these books away. I read only when I was alone, pausing every couple of pages to smooth out the spine, the cover. I sipped at the story, slowly, slowly.

At sixteen I left school to work on a building site, half a mile down the hill from the Old Manor. The River Wharfe went gurgling by. We were renovating a council estate. Tenants were moved back into the houses we'd finished, even as others a hundred yards away were being ripped apart, gutted. I carried bricks, mixed concrete, clobbered old foundations with a sledgehammer. I'd replaced Carlos, a Spaniard who'd left to go back to Valencia, El Cid's one-time domicile. 'Trouble wi' Carlos,' said Fred, the chief labourer, 'were that he couldn't speak a word o' English. But by 'eck 'e could dig 'oles.' Fred pointed to one, eight feet deep, straight-sided, a perfectly square, indeed uncannily precise, hole. 'Watch thissen. They're all over. Carlos were quarrying for summat but he never let on what. Or mebbe he did, but we couldn't mek 'im out.'

Fred had sandy-red hair, stiff as a brush. In his late twenties he'd married a doctor's pretty daughter. She expected more, so each day Fred made a diligent study of the *Daily Telegraph* job pages. 'Oh aye. I see they're after a chief executive officer on Liverpool District Council. I'll be 'aving that.' Or: 'Brain surgeons required in Edinburgh. I'll be greeted with open arms up there.'

Lunch and tea breaks were taken in the living-room of whichever house was nearest completion. The labourers sat on one side of the room, higher paid piece workers – plumbers, carpenters, plasterers – on the other. The division was happy enough, a truce helped along by the tacit agreement that, though the skilled workers earned perhaps five times as much, the labourers were allowed to steal whatever they could from the site. Baths went, timber, plaster, and bricks by the ton. My mother was surprised one afternoon when Fred and a couple of the crew turned up to replace our cracked kitchen window. 'Young Richard sent us,' Fred said. 'From down the road.' I'd told him that my father was the gardener at the Old Manor. I'd also told him that I was going to university, though I'd lied, saying Nottingham. I helped Fred with his job applications. I wrote a letter threatening legal action for a carpenter who took a spill into one of Carlos's creations. If all the plastering had been finished, the plasterers would come along, tip Fred twenty quid, and I'd be sent with a sledgehammer to smash in a wall so they could all set to again. 'Ruddy vandals,' Fred would explain to the foreman.

A cheerfully bent communism was at work. And something else too – throughout the day workmen disappeared into houses that had been finished, where the tenants had already moved back in. At first I didn't see; then I realized there were a lot of single mothers, not to mention housewives left alone by their husbands during the day.

'Oh aye, they're all at it,' said happily married Fred, meaning sex. I wanted to say: *Not me, I'm not.* I watched a roofer strolling up one of the garden paths. 'Come on then, Richard,' said Fred with a sigh. 'It's thee and me. The last true bastions of morality in a sad, sick world. We'll stick together then, eh?'

As a treat he persuaded the plasterers to teach me how to fill in and plaster a wall.

Three

Cambridge had been there centuries before me, would
continue long after I'd departed and been forgotten, but
while I was there it was mine. I was part of a vast,
cocooning fabric. I loved the bad sherry and dancing to
Abba at freshers' discos. Loved the rotten dinners which I
ate, gowned, in Emmanuel Hall. Loved spending too much
on a bike that was stolen almost at once, so I had to spend
too much on another. Loved my philosophy lectures:
Bernard Williams, boyish and brilliant, apologizing
because he was having an off day; Casimir Lewy, who'd
known Wittgenstein, wheezing and cackling: 'Of course
two and two is four, it's quite clear, quite obvious, unless
of course you are an ... *Ogggsford* logician.' I loved
Cambridge by day in the rain, a sandstone Eden, dripping
and dank; loved Cambridge at night, when fog came out
of the ground and rolled knee high off the river, when the
paving stones in Emmanuel Front Court were wet as if fog
rose from within to moisten their surface and the baby
spruce trees around the duck pond looked like cowled

12

monks. Loved lying drunk in bed at three, four in the morning as the college bells debated the hour. Emmanuel, Christ's, King's, counting out each its own different time.

This was 1974. It was easy to fit in. On the one hand there was King's College, where students still wore kaftans, took drugs, and toted copies of Marx and Marcuse. On the other there was Magdalene, home to sons of the aristocracy, squirey types in tweed jackets, some of whom, only five years later, would be young MPs in Margaret Thatcher's first government. In between it was possible to be anything. There was Roddy, who slept in a blue blazer and was the grandson of a Lord Justice of Appeal, and there was Jimmy, working class, a comedian from Liverpool who reeled off not just Monty Python but Lenny Bruce, Laurel and Hardy, Buster Keaton, even obscure vaudevillians like Arthur Askey, prancing about as he sang, 'Wot, no milk, dear-dear-dear-dear-dear.' There was Tom, who'd been born again while living in a Birmingham bedsit. A previous tenant had given the landlady a record-player on which, every night, she'd played *The Mikado*. She'd had only the one opera, but Tom had been driven into the arms of the Lord by both Gilbert *and* Sullivan.

I felt the stirrings of escape. My mother and stepfather had driven me down from Yorkshire, leaving me with my bags in Emmanuel Front Court, facing the chapel built by Sir Christopher Wren. I was taken over to my rooms, where, for some reason, my name hadn't been painted yet alongside all the rest at the bottom of the staircase.

My mother reported that, as they were driving away, she'd seen me walking back from the newsagent's, lugging a copy of the *Sunday Times* and a jumbo size bottle of Coca-Cola. I'd looked a little forlorn, she said. But after a week I was able to tell her I was quite at home. After two I felt as if I'd been in Cambridge all my life. My life hadn't started until the moment I walked through the Emmanuel gate and stood on the smooth, uneven stones within the cloisters.

I had an academic tutor, a personal tutor, and a moral tutor. The morality man was dean of the college, tall, with big ears and a drooping horselike face. He mentioned Wittgenstein's *Tractatus Logico-Philosophicus*, which I bought and praised and couldn't understand. At his recommendation I also toiled through *Principia Ethica* by G. E. Moore. The prose was clear, the ideas less so, but when I told him I was having trouble with ethics there was a forced, awkward moment. He stepped up on to Front Court's immaculate lawn, on which undergraduates were not allowed to set foot. 'In the intellectual rather than the practical sense, I trust,' he said, and exploded in a nervous gale of laughter.

Recently, when Paivi asked who had taught me about right and wrong, I answered *Why, no one*, for a moment astonished by the question, by the idea that anyone received useful tuition of that sort. I grew up, not necessarily with the belief but with the feeling, powerfully impressed on me, that life was a question of surviving, of making it through, not getting caught. I was like the

Spartan boy in the story, with the hidden fox gnawing at his insides.

My personal tutor, on the other hand, was assured and confident, insincere, a plump little pontiff whose academic speciality was the French Revolutionary Terror. He'd been an undergraduate at Emmanuel, had done his research there, had become a junior don, and, at last, a tenured fellow. I saw him once step outside the college gates. He stood quite still for several seconds, blinking, as if he needed to fortify himself before venturing to proceed. In his rooms he smoked French cigarettes between the V of his first and second fingers. Each puff was a little kiss. 'Now take Professor Wilson,' he said – kiss, kiss. 'The only time *he* has an orgasm is when he finds an old book.' He served gin, sherry, or whisky, depending on when I visited. Whisky was reserved for late at night, when there was a possibility that he'd make a pass or offer a job in British intelligence. The story around Emmanuel was that he recruited for MI5.

On my first morning a blue-rinsed woman in pink wellington boots had presented herself at the door and announced in a pert Scottish voice: 'I'm Mrs Swiggins. I'll be your bedder, dearie.' I'd read, in various descriptions of university life, that Cambridge students had little old ladies who made their beds and fussed over them in the morning. I hadn't quite accepted any part of this idea, which now turned out to be true. Mrs Swiggins had shoulders like a linebacker and hoovered the bed while I was still in it. 'Get up,' she said, 'get up and do some work, you lazy wee rascal.' Mrs Swiggins had dealt with many generations of turbulent male hormones. Walking in to discover me naked, she didn't bat an eye, but marched to the window, opened it, and shouted to a colleague in the quad below. 'Will you come and take a peek? He doesnae have any clothes on.'

MI5, servants, somehow none of it was surprising; it was Cambridge. In lectures I took my seat at the back and fumed about the long-haired beatnik who always seemed to be hogging the attentions of the Sue Barrand-like blonde from King's. 'As George was saying to me just yesterday,' he said one time, bragging of his latest conversation with a superstar don, 'we know that Heidegger applied the term metamorals to *just* this kind of rationalization. Of *course* morals are not a relative quality but one of primary being.'

I was sceptical of ideologies and rhetoric. I had opinions on every subject, could argue any position, and believed in almost nothing. I wasn't especially interested in politics. When people told me that England was, and always had been, in the throes of class war to the death I listened with a smile. I wasn't waiting for an enormous revolution. I was waiting for romantic love, which would fall on me like an Alp. My ideas of art and beauty came from Blake, Byron, and Emily Brontë, not to mention the gorgeous third movement of Mahler's 6th Symphony, which I'd stolen from the public library back in Yorkshire. Walking across Cambridge's Market Square, watching rain smudge the golden stone of King's College Chapel, I felt a huge relief, as if all of a sudden I'd been given my place in the world. I was waiting for happiness, and at Cambridge I was happier than I'd ever been.

I met Tony on the first night. 'Fancy a beer?' he said, initiating an intimacy that would last my three Cambridge years and beyond. Tony was tall, slender, a medical student; in his rooms there was a portrait he'd done of Keith Richards, a hollow-cheeked splatter of black ink. Tony's own features were smooth and round, like a cherub's. 'I envy Keith his face, not just his rhythm-guitar,' he said.

It was to Tony that I first confessed my ambition. The chess games we played, meeting at midnight, were excuse to bask in our dreams. He'd be Picasso and Keith Richards rolled into one. I'd be one part Evelyn Waugh, the other William Burroughs, a spectacular butterfly. We talked about what it might mean to be an artist. One had to be true to oneself, one's vision. Not sell out or do hack work.

'Look at Mozart, a *court* composer,' he said. 'That would make me puke.'

'Quite,' I said. I quite agreed; one didn't want to end up fudging it like Mozart.

Later, when Tony qualified as a surgeon, the Rolling Stones provided operating table accompaniment. He never had to try to pick up women. He stood at the bar with an angelic smile and waited for them to come to him. Since they usually came in twos or threes, I found myself meeting more than I ever had. Stumbling back from various pubs, the Eagle, with its Elizabethan gallery and cobbled courtyard, or the Rose, favoured because nurses from the old Addenbrookes Hospital went there, I felt the fog tingle and condense on my eyelids, making rainbows.

I can't remember when I first met Pete, a self-consciously cool figure in boots, jeans, and black velvet jacket. A Wykehamist, he smoked Marlboros, had met Harold Pinter, and contrived to carry himself like a debonair Latin American revolutionary. He had a moustache, a selection of silk scarves, a beret. His eyes always narrowed a little as he cupped his hand to light up the next fag. His parents, I learned as the weeks went by, had a flat in Mayfair, an estate in Norfolk. There was talk of 'the house in Chelsea', which had been bought for the kids. Peter Sellers lived next door. Yet he wore all this very easily. Opulence was displayed only by the delivery to his rooms of boxloads of salt 'n' vinegar crisps. His father, a refugee who'd fled Czechoslovakia penniless in 1937, now ran, amongst much else, the company that owned the company that made Golden Wonder. Pete had a poise, Tony a graciousness that was tremendously appealing. Pete was cool, Tony deliberately wasn't, and they both had something I clearly lacked: glamour.

Pete talked about a garden they had on the estate in Norfolk. It was entered through a wooden door painted white. On the other side, surrounded by walls of centuries-old pale red brick, were apple trees, pear trees, plum trees, beds for strawberries in the summer, and greenhouses where his Uncle Jack grew the plumpest, sweetest tomatoes you'd ever taste. Pete said he wasn't interested in any of the Cambridge women – he had a girlfriend in Norfolk who came to visit most weekends. When we went to the pubs he wasn't even on the look out. Tony stood there with his little smile, seemingly irresistible. It was left to me to be eager and bounce around and tell lots of jokes, aching with the certainty that I'd never find that bloody door.

At the end of that Christmas term I went with Pete to Chelsea. His family's house there, the one next door to Peter Sellers, was squashed and narrow, but seemed to go up for ever: five, six floors. The rooms themselves were like little boxes, all different shapes and sizes, some with angled ceilings, others with curving white plaster walls. There was a girl staying in the room next to mine. I met her when I went upstairs to unpack and a face popped around the door. 'Oh, so you're here,' she said. Red hair, pale skin – that was as much as I had the chance to take in. There was a shout from below.

'Rayner!'

Pete had decided to buy a suit. His sisters – and the other women in the house, of whom there seemed to be many, not just the redhead – heaped scorn. The suit was very expensive; he had no cash; probably the shop wasn't still open; altogether the idea was too ridiculous.

The redhead glanced at me from the end of the room,

next to the record-player. She seemed to want me to go over there, or so I hoped, but then Pete, who'd been on the phone, fingered his Zapata moustache and said, 'Rayner, we're off.'

We jumped in a cab and ten minutes later we were on Piccadilly, sashaying through swing doors into the Ritz. There was an atmosphere of peace, of reverence almost. The carpet was thick and springy, taking into itself all the noise of London, leaving a pleasant murmur and babble. A soft golden light came from chandeliers. People glided by, dressed in tuxedos and evening gowns, pulling on white silk scarves and coats ready for dinner, the theatre, the night ahead. A uniformed concierge came bustling towards us, white envelope in left hand. I was certain we were going to be thrown out.

'*Mr Peter*,' announced the concierge, delighted. 'How nice, how *wonderful* to see you again, sir.' He handed Pete the envelope, stuffed with five and ten pound notes. 'Please do come and see us again, sir, and give my best to Sir Joseph and Lady Joseph.'

We rushed out again into the cold December night. I hailed another cab, and we made it back to the King's Road as the shop was closing. Pete asked them to stay open, carrying all this off, not with self-mockery, but as though it were quite ordinary, nothing special. He stood in front of a mirror wearing the suit, which was of gorgeous deep bottle-green velvet – price two hundred and fifty guineas.

'My parents used to keep a suite there,' he said, meaning the Ritz.

I wasn't envious. I was dazzled.

The next evening there was a dinner party in the living-room, so tiny and neat it resembled the inside of a doll's house. Beforehand women darted about in various states of undress. I wasn't sure which were Pete's sisters and which not; he eyed them all with the same cool disdain, then asked how they liked his new suit.

I was seated next to the redhead from upstairs. Her eyes were bloodshot as if she'd been crying. She talked to me about her boyfriend, an Italian film actor named Franco. Her father disapproved. He himself was a writer turned film star, a famous talent, tyrant, and nutcase. He didn't want her involved with show business or anyone connected with it.

'We just had the most bloody awful row,' she said. 'Daddy's such a stinker.' She sighed. 'What about yours?'

'He's dead.'

She looked at me as if noticing me for the first time and touched my sleeve with her hand. 'I'm sorry,' she said.

'Happened a long time ago, cancer,' I said, and we started to get on well. I recited a couple of poems by Blake, a new tactic.

Afterwards, hunting for more wine in the kitchen, Pete asked, 'What's this about your father being dead?'

My heart gave a bump. All through school I'd wished that my father were dead, though we didn't know for sure; so I'd made up stories about who my father was and what he did. The stories had laid it on thick about how boring and mundane he was, and how he lived in some far distant country – hot, like Bahrain, which was why he never came to visit. I'd never told the truth, I thought I'd be annihilated if anyone ever found out, and I'd carried on lying at Cambridge, telling Pete something else, that my father was up in Yorkshire, a novelist turned publishing executive. I'd told him, in effect, that my *stepfather* was my father.

'Oh, it was such a long time ago,' I said, facing Pete in the kitchen of the house in Chelsea. 'He died just after I was born. I've always thought of my stepfather as if he were my father.'

Pete shrugged. 'It's good that you get on with him so well.'

I had to lean against the door for a moment. I was rubbery with fear and relief – as if someone had burst into my soul with a camera.

The next term Pete and I announced that we were forming a theatre company. The college duly handed over five hundred pounds. Five hundred quid, no questions asked – it was funny money, and our first move was to catch the train to London for an appropriately directorial lunch. After that Pete did David Hare, I went for Joe Orton, and Tony's smile became even more than usually angelic as he blew the rest of the budget on crates of Löwenbräu for a last night party.

I was at the soothing centre of things. Our Welsh friend Danny had told us about this gorgeous girl he slept with from time to time, Kathy, who was visiting for the weekend. But in the pub before the final performance it was obvious she and Danny knew each other hardly at all. For once I saw a woman not as a target to be flattered and impressed but as someone with a problem. I asked where she was from in Wales. I remembered a few phrases of the Welsh I'd learned as a kid. I asked about her parents. Joke-telling did not break out like an uncontrollable case of acne. I bought a round of drinks, then Tony, Pete, and I left for the performances, after which there was the party. Danny and Kathy appeared, still arguing. 'Hell!' said Danny. 'You don't think I invited you all the way from Cardiff just so I could sleep with you, do you?' Pete and I basked in the glory of our brief flurry as theatrical impresarios. Tom was there, my evangelist Pooh Bah friend. At the sight of Tony – who was on his hands and knees like a dog, panting, licking at a pool of spilled beer which was disappearing into the carpet – he was moved to point, not at Tony, but at me: 'You're lost,' he warned, 'you're a lost soul.'

When I got back to my rooms Kathy was sitting on the end of the bed. I tried not to feel too smug.

Granny Michie, my stepfather's mother, was enormously tall, with hanging bloodhound jowls and long flippers for feet. Her temper was all shoes and elbows. She treated her adult sons as though they were small children, calling their wives, and thus my mother, 'trollops', 'sluts', and 'fisher-women'. This Albert Memorial of a woman was foul to me most of the time, but punishingly accurate. 'You think of no one but yourself,' she said, and 'horrible, so horrible', and 'arrogant selfish boy'.

I was back at the Old Manor for Easter. On the morning of the annual Boat Race between Oxford and Cambridge she came into the living-room and asked in a quite different, a shy, almost girlish voice if I'd mind putting something on the record-player. We listened for a half-hour to Elgar's Cello Concerto, the famous Barbirolli recording with Jacqueline du Pré. I was swept along by the music's sumptuous sadness and passion, its abandonment of restraint.

'Do you like it?' she asked.

I told her, very much.

'I hoped you would,' she said, beaming. 'It's yours. I bought it for you.'

We settled down to watch the race together. She fussed about in her chair, while I posed on the couch, fortified by the Elgar and feigning cool. 'Really,' I said. 'We're above this kind of thing at Cambridge. Only dumb hearties take rowing seriously at all.'

'Come on, Oxford,' she said. 'Trounce them!' She understood better than anyone in my own family the romance of Cambridge and the real consequences Cambridge might entail. Cambridge was status, with the promise of position and power, a golden future down the river. Neither of her boys had been there, or to Oxford for that matter, and none of her grandchildren. 'Come on the Dark Blues!' she said, leaning forward, really getting into it.

This was the year Cambridge sank.

'Nasty,' she said, as the waters of the Thames frothed over the gunwales, and the boat began to go down, taking the bemused Cambridge eight with it. 'Nasty Cambridge cheats. And your father is a crook.'

Edward Bertram Rayner, my father's father, was born at the turn of the century. He was tall and fair, with a hook nose – the Rayner beak, my mother calls it. A drinker, a womanizer, yet seemingly ambitious, a chancer, he surprised everybody by turning round and marrying a shop girl, an Irish Catholic from County Cork.

Bert Rayner loved to swim. His wife, my Nanna Wrose, called him 'the water baby'. After a late summer holiday in Blackpool, when the water had already turned cold, and during which he'd swum and dived often, he complained of a bad earache. Instead of getting treatment he carried on down to London, for the Motor Show at Earl's Court, and, by the time he came back to Yorkshire, the earache was meningitis. He died within a few days. He was thirty at the time, my father ten.

In all the years I knew her Nanna Wrose never spoke of this. I never once heard her complain or raise her voice about anything. She'd spoiled my father, adored him, and even when he vanished, there was no question of reproach. She was always a great friend, a rock, to my mother and me.

'He's alive,' she said. 'I know he is. I feel it in my blood. You think so too, don't you, Richard.'

Nanna Wrose was dying from cancer. Her skin had a sheen, like wax, and her face was so emaciated the eyes seemed to pop right out. Her black hair, usually kept up in a bun, was spread out on the pillow, oddly youthful and abundant.

I made tea and read to her from the Bible. She pressed my fingers between her own.

I'd spent I don't know how many scores of nights in that room. It had always been cold and damp, and I'd bury myself in the mattress, blankets up to my nose, hot-water bottle tight between my knees. I'd imagine that I was camping out in a jungle somewhere, with the reassurance that Nanna and Grandad were a few yards away. It was cold and damp still, though that sense of innocent reassurance had vanished. Reckless, already in debt at Cambridge, I'd gone to them – not my mother and stepfather – for money, and they'd sent a cheque they couldn't afford.

She said, 'You want to see him again, don't you?'

A drop of condensation meandered down the window. 'Yes, Nan,' I lied. 'I'd like to see him.'

Her grip tightened. 'You love him, you see. You'll always love your dad.'

I was back at Cambridge when she died two months later, towards the end of the summer term. My mother called me. The funeral was at Nab Wood, a red brick crematorium at the bottom of a hill outside Bradford. Most of my family is buried there. The place has no attractive or comforting feature; well, perhaps one – from outside the Chapel of Rest you can catch a glimpse of the moors' purple heather above Haworth.

I saw him as soon as I got out of the car, twenty feet away, crunching across the gravel: my father, dressed in prison grey. He was older, thinner, much the same. He was talking to a man I didn't know, one of the undertakers. 'Hello, Richard,' he said, quite matter-of-factly. We shook hands. His jacket was made of a stiff fabric with prickles and it came only as far as the waist, like the ones Winston Churchill used to wear. 'Sad day.'

I felt no pleasure, no anger, nothing much; there he is, I thought, my dad. After the service he located the family plot, where his mother was to be buried, and then he was gone, between two prison guards in the back of a van.

I'd always known in my heart he'd show up one day, the ghost who decided to step back into his former life. There'd been rumours – he'd been seen, in Leeds, in Bradford, at the Oddfellows' Arms in Shipley, a favourite pub. There'd been Granny Michie's jibe on the morning of the Boat Race, but I'd been hoping, praying it wasn't true.

As a child I'd soon realized that my father wasn't like other fathers. He loved cricket and worked the way people seemed to work in the movies – not a lot. He had a thin moustache, an air of suave indifference borrowed from Fred Astaire or David Niven, and he was interested in any woman who wasn't my mother. He was often away from home, and during these unexplained absences the police would come to our house, asking if we knew where he was. I must have been three or four when he told my mother that he was going out for a pint of milk. He came back two weeks later with a bottle in each hand, saying, 'I got two, just to be on the safe side.' Another early memory: I was with him in a Mini Cooper S, a small and very fast car of the 1960s. My father had competed in the Monte Carlo Rally and was a skilled driver – he never did get along with speed limits. On this occasion he grinned, nodding in the direction of the speedometer, which said 105 m.p.h., and took his hands from the wheel. He sang, 'Yes, we have no bananas, we have no bananas today.'

It was in 1962 that we moved from Yorkshire to live in the seaside resort of Llandudno, and it was in December of that year that my mother left him at last, winter boots crunching through the snow. She never came back and he never quite got over it. For a while he tried to buckle down. He owned a garage and various other small businesses, including a coffee bar he called Boz after Dickens's pen-name early on. His favourite characters were Bill Sikes and, of course, Mr Micawber. But pretty quickly he had debts and was in trouble with the police. People were after him, he said, and not just in Llandudno; they were on their way down from Bradford as well. He cried about my mother. I hated him for being drunk, not understanding how desperate he was. One night, when I was on holiday from the boarding school, I went into his bedroom and found a mountain of banknotes on a table. They were so crisp and new they creaked gently in a draught from the door. It was soon after this that he'd vanished.

Now Jack – Flash Jack, Black Jack, Jack the Lad – was back. When my sister Helen and I went to see him in prison the walls in the visitors' room were slick and shiny grey, sealed with magnesite paint. The floor was covered with the same substance. Everything was warm and moist, clammy to the touch. Pipes were steaming all around like revealed intestines.

A wall of security glass ran above a counter at the end of the room. This was where we sat. Prison guards looked down from a gantry above our heads.

A door opened to the side of the gantry and six prisoners were marched down the steps. My father sat down and we spoke to him through a Perspex grille. He wasn't trying to smile. He looked pale and frightened. He talked about the woman he'd been living with when the police had caught up with him. She was Scottish, with two grown-up sons.

'Her name's Connie and she's a very classy lady. You'll like her,' he said, daring us to contradict him.

All the while I was thinking, what am I doing, why am I here? No one in the family seemed to find it odd that he'd turned up or if they did the issue was never discussed. Yet I'd got the sense from all of them – my brother, my sister, my mother as well – that they thought I should get to know him again. Why? He'd never been a rule-making, home-ruling, let's-go-to-the-park provider and authority figure. I had my own life and didn't need him.

'Is it rotten, Dad?' my sister asked. He was on remand, awaiting trial, and this was Armley, one of the worst gaols in the country.

'Not so bad,' he said, with a smile and a shrug, but there were tears in his eyes. 'I hear you're at Cambridge now,' he said, turning to me. 'That's great. I'm very proud of you. What's it like?'

'Good,' I said, 'fine.'

'Lots of the right sort of people,' he said. 'Do yourself well there and you'll be set up for life. Great opportunity.'

'I suppose,' I said.

'Mark my words,' he said.

'Thanks,' I said, wanting to change the subject. Not wasted on me, I thought, the irony of this sad, smiling father presuming to advise his son on the educational advantages of Cambridge – here, in Armley, rubbing shoulders with the murderers, the rapists.

A guard called that visiting time was over. At last I felt able to breathe.

My memories of the rest of that summer? Are of 10cc's 'I'm Not in Love', and my own fruitless attempts to be so. Girls seemed to avoid me in some mysterious way. In a Marbella discotheque two were swept away by the footballer George Best; or, rather, it was his minder who did the sweeping, delivering them to a booth of orange plush where George sat, bearded, running a little to seed, and sipping a Piña Colada. This became my stock anecdote for the next couple of months: bizarrely unlucky in love.

About my father I said nothing, and nothing further was said to me. He'd been gone, he was back, he was the same old skeleton in the closet, his presence as ghostly as his absence had been. His war record had been mentioned at the trial, which had taken place soon after Nanna Wrose's funeral. There were a couple of brief stories in the national press, and he was transferred to a minimum security prison. Helen and I went to visit him again. His girlfriend Connie was there this time, a woman of such poise she could walk through a Glasgow slum attracting neither insult nor even a speck of dirt to spoil the perfection of her Chanel suit. She was tall, with large eyes, and she wore lilac gloves, one of which she took off to hold my hand.

My father had recovered some of his old zest and twinkle. His bushy eyebrows soared up and down as he told stories about the other prisoners, all of whom, he said, were harmless white-collar crooks like himself: fraudulent clergymen, journalists who'd done something a little too spectacular with the expenses. Since he didn't smoke he'd been able to set himself up with a nice little business trading tobacco rations. Snout, he called it. The prison, fifty or so corrugated-iron Nissen huts, had been in its former life an RAF base; he'd been stationed here for a few months during the war.

'Funny, eh?' he said, meaning not funny at all.

Should I give him a kiss and a hug? I imagined that I bore no grudge. I felt pleased with myself for having come at all, proving the good son I was, and, by implication, the rotten father he'd been. At the trial he'd pleaded guilty to everything of which Richard Evans had accused him all those years ago. He'd embezzled a large amount of money and faked his own death. He'd fled, first to South America, and, later, South Africa. This much I already knew, and I wasn't interested in trying to find out any more.

Four

It was at the beginning of the next Cambridge year. Pete and I were walking in the street when we met a friend of his, an acquaintance from Norfolk, one of those squirey types with a green tweed hunting jacket and not much chin: Henry. Afterwards Pete asked me how I'd liked him.

'Oh, he's boring,' I said.

Pete turned. 'Boring?' he said with venom. 'He's more interesting that you'll *ever* be.'

It stung. I knew his reaction had something to do with Norfolk, and the special quality of his life there, though I didn't see at the time the extent to which he himself must have had different worlds which he kept in fragile orbit. I thought it was all about me, and perhaps it was. I remember looking at myself in the mirror. Was I really so bland and characterless?

That year was all Janie. I met her at one of those freshers' discos Pete, Tony, and I were far too mature and sophisticated to bother with but which, somehow, we went to anyway. I feel I should remember the record that was playing when I first saw her. 'Waterloo'? 'Stairway to Heaven'? 'Suffragette City'? I don't know. But there she was, in a white dress with flowers on it, a slender athletic-looking girl with curling brunette hair and blue eyes. She was surrounded by boys. Even Tony, whose judgement in these matters had the authority of Berenson, agreed that she'd more than do.

At first Janie and I saw each other only once or twice a week. Later, after we'd made love, she said that during all this time she'd carried on seeing lots of those other boys. There was X from King's, Y from Selwyn, Des the Magdalene tennis ace. Janie was a nifty tennis player herself.

It hadn't occurred to me she might be seeing even one other; just as well – I'd have been destroyed. My silence was interpreted as evidence of cool. 'I chose you,' Janie said, and I snuggled up, her first. I let her believe I was a lot more experienced than I was.

We were together every second of every day. Even the comic moments were enchanting. Janie's friends made excuses to come into her room in the morning. They peeped around the door, giggling. Such evidence of feminine immaturity, as opposed to my own, was very beguiling. Sometimes they brought cups of tea, with chocolate digestives on a tray, and me sitting up in Janie's bed like Little Lord Fauntleroy.

Mostly it was all very serious. I fretted whenever she was out of my sight. Jealousy burst forth if someone came to talk to her in a pub or admired her graceful backhand on the tennis court. One morning I announced sternly: 'I'm going to be a writer.' Janie agreed that this was a terrific idea.

I told her my father had died in a car crash when I'd been eight. He'd been on his way back from a cricket match. The irony was that he was such a good driver – professional rally standard. Perhaps it had been the car, I said, a black pre-war Citroën he'd borrowed from a pal. The Gestapo car, he'd called it.

'Oh, Rich,' Janie said. 'That must have been terrible.'

I agreed that it had been bad.

Very bad: it was no strain saying all this, even to her. I quite believed in the lie as I was telling it and was unbothered by the fact that I'd told Pete a different one. There was no conflict. The sections of my life were a puzzle easier to keep apart than put together. Only the one thing was certain, I thought: they'd never meet up. There was no danger of that.

As for Janie's parents, I got on with them well enough. Her father was red faced, a businessman, cheerful and bluff. He liked messing about in boats. Her mother was a different proposition. Chairwoman of the local Conservative Party, she carried with her the air of bloody battles fought, and victories triumphantly gained, on all the hockey fields of the Home Counties. They combined to convey the impression that I wasn't the worst nightmare their daughter might have come home with, and when they suggested that the two of us join them for a holiday it seemed really rather a good idea. Janie and I would be together, she'd be fulfilling family obligations, and after that we'd take the rest of the summer as arranged: I'd be working as an intern with a big firm of West End lawyers, and travelling each weekend down to Cornwall, where Janie would be teaching. So we said yes, to a fortnight with Janie's parents and their dogs in Scotland. In a caravan.

It was the first of the long hot summers of the mid-1970s, but not in Scotland. Each day was oppressive with clouds, thunder. We drove long and far in a Volvo with the windows up and Janie's father drumming his fingers on the wheel. In the back I tried to slide my own fingers up Janie's wrist. 'DON'T HOLD HANDS!' he screamed. Lunch was a sandwich and a half-pint of shandy. After dinner there was Scottish folk dancing. Janie's parents were very keen on Scottish folk dancing.

Once they did leave us alone with the dogs. They'd been gone for ten minutes when I heard the Volvo bouncing, sloshing, racing back towards the caravan across the ruts and mud of the camp site. Janie and I were out of breath, panting and barely dressed, when her mother popped her head around the door. It wasn't just the dancing tonight, she said, but pipers too, all the way from Edinburgh. She answered my sulk with a superb hockey-stick swish.

'You know what you are, Rich? You're a snob.'

Slowly we made our way over to the east coast, where a weekend was to be spent with friends. I saw a road sign to Nairn and, once we'd arrived at the friends' house, I excused myself, made a phone call from a box at the end of the street, and hopped on a bus.

My father threw his arm around my shoulder and hugged me tight. 'Great to see you, son,' he said. He was dressed in a blue blazer, white polo-neck, and slacks, as if he'd stepped off a nearby yacht. 'Thought you'd surprise the old man in his new abode, eh?'

Connie's hotel was a substantial Victorian affair, red brick, with six floors and three stars from the Automobile Association. My father had taken over the running of the place. As we talked in the bar people came and went – the chef, the manager, one of the receptionists, all treated with the same smiling offhand confidence. This was another side of him I'd forgotten. He could run a business.

Two men joined us at our table, Graham and Geoffrey, Connie's adult sons. One was bald, the other bespectacled, both in their thirties and dourly Scottish, stern as Nairn itself. They glanced at me and shook hands, but for the most part kept their eyes on my father, who was telling a story. They watched him closely, perhaps afraid he was about to run off with the spoons.

My father had met Connie on a cruise ship, somewhere between Cape Town and Durban. By then he'd been in South Africa three or four years, money all gone long before that. She was a widow, attractive, and he was ready for a change from his job selling real estate, ready perhaps to fall in love, though I never imagined him fretting much over romance. He was too cagey and practical. He had a confident briskness with women, but his dreams lay in other areas. His charm, his warmth and good humour made him a terrific companion, and you never quite knew where you stood with him. He'd never let you find his edges.

He decided to quit South Africa and come with Connie back to England. She bought a shop in a Derbyshire village and the two of them set up together in antiques. Selling – he was always good at that, and soon the two of them were travelling all over the country. Business had taken them to Bradford, where he'd been spotted, and then, in Derbyshire, there had been the knock on the door. He'd been in prison for a little more than a year, and Connie had waited.

A party had been arranged in my honour, upstairs in Connie's flat. There was whisky and champagne, and hotel maids spun about with trays of sandwiches, sausage rolls, and smoked salmon on little triangles of brown bread. Connie took me by the cheeks and told me I had heart-breaker's eyes. 'A toast,' my father said, summoning everyone to their feet. He smiled his barmy smile. 'To Richard, my son.' He kept putting his arm around me and saying we had to chat about things, but before any such discussion could get underway he'd press another glass into my hand, take me by the elbow, and introduce me to some new friend. My presence was confirmation of something that had been in doubt – that he had a family, a past, an existence he hadn't made up. Graham and Geoffrey loitered on the fringe, drinking hard, twin Banquos at the feast.

'I want you to know,' my father said to me, 'that I came back to find my children.'

I was drunk. I nodded, saying I knew that.

He was drunk as well. 'I came back to find you,' he said, and gave me a hug. 'I'm sorry, son.'

Late that night, when the party was over, I found a diamond ring in the bathroom. Connie must have been getting ready for bed and left it there, in the soap dish, a gold band with six or seven stones set in a line and a cluster of three more at the centre. Worth thousands, I thought, and the impulse was sudden as rage: take it, sell it.

My fingers were slippery with soap as I took the ring from the dish. They'd never suspect, and, even if they did, I knew, they'd never accuse. I turned off the light and stood there for what seemed like hours. The bathroom window, twin panes of frosted glass, glowed and sparkled yellow with light diffused from a street lamp. An ambulance went by. I put the ring back.

At first Janie refused to talk. She swept aside my apologies and wouldn't let me touch her. At last she said: 'Where did you go? What happened to you? My parents are furious – I feel so humiliated. Where *were* you?'

I asked if she remembered what I'd told her about my father.

'Of course,' she said, 'the car crash.'

'It was a lie,' I told her. 'I've just been to see him. He's alive.' This was the moment for the whole truth. I knew.

We were outside in the garden of the house of her parents'
friends. I saw Janie's mother staring at us, expressionless,
from the kitchen window. Bees were buzzing, there was
the smell of roses.

'He's ill,' I said. 'Really sick. I had to go.'

I'd been at the law firm a week. The case involved two
defendants, a spiv who was accused of stealing cars and
car radios, and a police constable alleged to have received
one of the radios as a bribe to let the spiv off the hook.
The heat was numbing, the case at the Old Bailey a simple
one. The spiv was very obviously *very* guilty. The prosecution knew, the defence knew, the jury knew, and the
judge, Justice Scott, *certainly* knew – he was going to gaol.
The spiv himself knew this: he made jokes and faces, and
was dressed in a snazzy pinstripe suit. Justice Scott, sitting
on high dressed in red and white robes with the insignia of
state behind him and a powdered wig on his head, listened
to this portion of the trial with, mostly, a bored disdain.
Often he seemed on the point of falling asleep, and once
he actually did, then snapped himself awake with a
practised motion.

The problem was the young constable. He was tall and
fair, very young, a Yorkshireman, like myself, who found
himself in London. He stood straight when called to
the witness stand. He spoke slowly and after much
thought, with a heavy accent. Obviously he was guilty as
well, and no one wanted him to be, because it became

clear that he'd been stupid and naive, not wilfully corrupt, and because, if convicted, he'd lose his job. A future was at stake, perhaps an entire life.

Justice Scott pretty much took over. Perhaps the young constable hadn't known of the presence of the radio in his living-room?

'Oh, no, yer 'onour, I knew it were there,' said the constable, after great deliberation.

Was it possible, then, just *possible*, mind, that the radio had been planted?

'No, yer 'onour, I know it weren't planted, 'cos I took it there meself.'

A sigh from Justice Scott. Wouldn't it be fair to say, wouldn't it be possible, just *possible*, again, that the constable hadn't known for sure that the radio was stolen?

The young constable didn't even have to lie very hard, Justice Scott was making it so easy for him. All he had to do was say he hadn't known for sure, and he'd be off the hook. Everyone in the court held their breath. The barrister for the defence stood quite still, easing his tongue out between his lips. Even the spiv was serious for a moment, wiping sweat from the back of his neck with a handkerchief.

'Oh, no, yer 'onour, I *knew* the radio were stolen,' said the young constable brightly.

Justice Scott sat back with an explosive sigh. He rolled his eyes at the ceiling, and, when all the rest of the evidence was in, turned to the jury and said: 'Well, you can't say I didn't try.' The spiv was sent down, five years for what turned out to be his umpteenth offence, and, though the young constable was given only a suspended sentence, he was automatically dismissed from the police force. He raised a hand to his parents at the back of the court, and then he was led away, looking shy and fragile.

I didn't feel wiser, or braver, or more optimistic after witnessing the legal system at work. I felt excited, though. The vivid theatricality with which it had all been staged, and in which all the professionals had participated with such gusto, contrasted so sharply with the murky moral issues involved. There'd been two sides in court, not defence and prosecution, but lawyers and everyone else, and I altogether fancied myself a barrister, acting away in wig and gown, or even, ultimately, an eccentric judge like Justice Scott – dispensing quips and judgement. A life had been in the balance and had been found lacking. I knew which side I wanted to be on.

I walked back towards Piccadilly, where the firm had its offices. London that summer seemed not like London at all, but a city on the Mediterranean, Marseilles or even Algiers, teeming and furious one moment, stunned the next in an exhausted torpor. A woman screamed at me; another greeted me, for no better reason, with a languid smile. People were dying in the heat. The city stank of rotting fruit left out in the street. Boxes of peaches turned to a sweet, sickly slush.

At the firm I sat down, writing yet another letter of apology to Janie, and was called in by Brian, the partner who'd arranged my internship. He was a small, heavy man in spectacles and sat behind a huge desk heaped up with files. The walls were lined with the black and tan volumes of the All England Law Reports and yet the office itself, eight floors up above Piccadilly behind a huge plate-glass window, seemed oddly airy and bright.

'Now,' said Brian. 'One of our clients has sent in a cheque for twenty-five thousand pounds by mistake.' He held up the cheque for me to inspect. 'He has, in fact, paid his bill twice, silly bugger. What do we do?' Brian heaved up his braces, smiling broadly.

'He's our own client?'

'Our own client.'

'A good client?'

'A good client,' Brian said. He had a fluting lawyerly voice, given to nuance and adjustment in emphasis. 'Not an *important* client.'

'Send it back,' I volunteered hopefully.

'No!' said Brian, banging an imaginary gong. I wondered if he was a little crazy. 'Incorrect answer. We do not send back the money. We never send back the money. We put the money we never send back in our deposit account and hold on to it until he notices that he's sent the money by mistake. And what do we do then?'

'Not send back the money?' I said, catching on.

'Good, good,' Brian said. 'We say, "Oh, of course what a terrible thing."'

'We'll have to check into it.'

'Which might take time.'

'Quite a long time.'

'Perhaps a *very* long time, until, at last, the confusion is resolved, and by then hopefully he'll be apologizing to us for having caused so much inconvenience.' He waved a hand – here endeth the lesson.

I thought about money. I'd never had much and fancied lots. Would I make it fast enough, I wondered, in the law? For three hours that afternoon, with no breeze at all coming through the opened window in my office, I wrote letters to various merchant banks and property developers. Perhaps they'd consider me for a position when I graduated? After that I went on with my letter of love and abject apology to Janie, and roughed out a scene of the novel I'd started.

I left the office and walked at random, thinking with my feet. I was a city boy now, for the first time in my life, and, as the heat of the day began to cool a little, London cast a different spell. It glowed in a soft haze. In the park people strolled in their shirtsleeves and took boats on the Serpentine. A fist fight started up outside South Kensington tube station for no reason anyone knew, perhaps only because the participants had suddenly found the energy to breathe. My future might be anything.

I was walking through West Kensington one night and went into the Nashville, where two or three bands played most evenings. Two microphones and a drum kit stood on the empty stage, and at the bar I found myself standing next to a fellow dressed in the most extraordinary costume

I'd ever seen. He wore army boots with no laces and red and black tartan trousers at the back of which a scrubby white cloth hung down. His white T-shirt had been slashed to ribbons with a razor and then put together again with safety pins. He had safety pins in his ear and the side of his nose. Another had been punched through his cheek, drawing one side of his mouth upwards. His dyed hair had been sculpted with mucus-like gook so it stood up in stiff orange spikes. I asked what the previous band had been like and he snarled: 'Six vodkas and limes, which is what Oi've just 'ad.'

This was my first experience of punk, and when the band started up, sounding like several steamrollers, I watched one girl wobbling on high heels with holes ripped in her fishnet stockings. She had one of those Statue of Liberty hair-dos. She bounced up and down, leaping towards the stage with her mouth wide open. It was a while before I realized that she was aiming herself, not at the singer, but at the gobs of spit he was raining down on the audience. She followed as the singer spat to the left and to the right, as he spat straight up in the air so it landed back in his own face; at the highest, slowest of his arcing gobs, she jumped, broke a heel, and supported herself on the shoulders of a friend before she snapped it up like a trout. The singer spat some more and shouted: 'NO FUTURE,' 'FUCK OFF,' and 'FUCK OFF, YOU WANKERS.'

A few days later the partner summoned me in again. The blinds were drawn in his airy office. One of the merchant banks I'd written to had called him and asked for a reference. Did I have any idea, he said, sighing, of the implications of using headed notepaper? That kind of thing could compromise the firm. He was sorry, but he had no choice but to let me go. He hitched up his braces. 'I really am sorry.'

My eyes burned. I got my things together and took the lift to the ground floor, where the doorman had been instructed to check inside my briefcase. Traffic honked on Piccadilly, rumbling through the treacly air. A red London bus was in trouble, stalled and fuming with its hinged bonnet thrown up and steam pouring out. I imagined myself beating the partner's face in. No future.

I caught the midnight train from Paddington to Penzance, sharing a compartment with three sailors, two men and a woman, all about my own age, who were going back to their ship in Exeter. They slammed down six-packs of Heineken and took swigs from a bottle of Johnnie Walker. I sat there, on fire with a different panic, determined not to move. The woman was blonde and strong looking, with blotches all over her face as if she'd been stung or scalded. She swore and drank as hard as the boys, harder. I was reading Christopher Sykes's biography of Evelyn Waugh. *Wanker*, I saw her thinking.

I assumed a thick Yorkshire accent. I asked if they knew where the prison was in Exeter. This got their interest. I explained that I was going to see my father. Bank robbery, I said, ten-year stretch. My knowledge of crime and prison was detailed enough for them to fall for it, and within a

few minutes the woman with the mottled face was offering
lager and whisky, as if I too were an old shipmate.

The rest of the summer was spent down in Cornwall with
Janie. During the day she went to teach at her school while
I did odd jobs around the camp site. We swam at night,
and during the weekends made trips to Land's End or the
witches' museum at Boscastle. It should have been a
blissful time, and I told myself it was, not knowing then
that people fall out of love and it happens at different
speeds. I was the anachronism.

Five

At the start of my third Cambridge year I panicked. I realized all of a sudden I had a life and was expected to do something with it. I felt that a career was in order and that a bad degree in philosophy wasn't going to help. I decided that despite the experience of the summer, my calling would after all be the law – ironic, given that I was my father's son, but then the irony passed me by, as irony usually did. So I switched my studies from philosophy, and, determined to make up for all the time I'd frittered away, I pored over the All England Law Reports, silently mouthing cases from tort and criminal law. I asked Janie to marry me – it all seemed to be part of the procedure, but she was angry because I hadn't thought the idea through, and then she was angry because I wasn't upset that she refused me.

Meanwhile my father – making resolves of his own, determined to be the good father and patriarch – came with Connie to visit. First of all he took me upstairs to their room at the University Arms Hotel, rooms rather, a suite with billowing white curtains and a balcony over-looking the fields of Parker's Piece. 'Not bad, eh?' he said with a wink, meaning not just the rooms, or the beauty of Cambridge, but both our situations. He wore an RAF tie and a double-breasted blazer. The brass buttons had little anchors on them. 'What do you say to a drink?'

I was thinking in terms of damage containment.

'Gin and it and two Famous Grouse when you've got a minute, Charlie,' he said to the barman. 'Large ones.'

The barman smiled at him as though they'd been friends all their lives. 'Coming right up, Squadron Leader,' he said.

My father's actual RAF rank had been Flight Sergeant. I thought: *How'd you do it? How do you do this and get away with it?* 'This is my son Richard,' he announced, not just to Charlie the barman, but the room at large. 'He's at the Varsity.'

Connie gazed on with a poise, a shrewd inner watchful-ness and calm. It was hard to know what she was thinking. She hadn't known a thing about my father's past. 'Didn't bat an eye,' he said of her reaction when she did hear, after his arrest. 'Coolest damn thing I ever saw.'

I was in a daze.

They wanted to see where I worked, where I drank and slept. They wanted to meet my friends. 'And what's this I hear about a certain lovely young lady? Janie,' he said, beaming. 'Where's the popsie?'

I was thinking to myself that everything would still be all right, that I'd give them a quick shimmy around

Emmanuel and shoo them on their way. It was mid-morning. All the others would be hard at work, I thought, but we were passing through the Front Court cloisters when I saw Tony and Pete coming towards us from the pond, ducks waddling behind. Pete had a blue silk scarf draped around his neck, while Tony, as usual, wore a far-away smile, as if listening to 'Gimme Shelter' on some inner stereo.

I wondered whether I should grab my father and steer him into the chapel but suddenly all the fight went out of me. It was happening with the dreamy inevitability of a car crash.

'Call me Jack,' he said. 'I'm Richard's dad.' He shook, first Tony's hand, and then Pete's, not letting go. 'What's absolutely the best place to eat in town?' Somehow he understood that Pete would know. Some radar he had swept in Pete's appearance and showed up money, class.

Bugger, bugger, I thought.

'That's settled then,' my father said. 'We'll all go there for dinner.'

As we walked back through Front Court I told him that Tony's father was a businessman, in electronics, while Pete's father was a millionaire executive, a knight of the realm. He was fascinated, of course. 'Nice boys,' he said, looking around at the chapel by Sir Christopher Wren. 'Lovely architecture.'

*

I thought I'd have to kill myself. Failing that, I thought, I'll fake my death, and leave my own pile of clothes next to a convenient body of water – the Cam would do. I spent the rest of the day squirming. I thought about skipping town, forgetting about my father, my friends and my degree, forgetting even about Janie, with whom things had been getting worse. So instead I used this as an opportunity to visit her and make my plea. My father – suddenly recovered – had put in an unexpected appearance and wanted to see us both for dinner. She took it well. She was actually pleased: we laughed, made love, and I began to see that Dad might have his uses.

That night I put on the blue suit, my only suit, bought for me by my mother from Freeman's, a mail order club. The suit wasn't made from cotton, or wool, or any of the potentially excellent synthetic fabrics, but some material that seemed actually to have been woven together out of cardboard. Yet the cut was highest fashion: a garment of surging lapels and great flapping flares, this was a suit almost too sharp to be true, and stiff, unbending to the touch. 'Oh dear,' my mother had said, lifting it gingerly out of the box. Coming from Bradford, she knew her cloth. 'This is a mistake, isn't it?' It fell about the body like armour.

I had stories ready for Pete. I'd blame the suit on my mother, and if he asked about Jack I was going to say that this was my *stepfather*, who, as I'd previously told him, I'd always thought of as my father, and it was all rather embarrassing because it seemed that he'd *left* my mother and taken up with a Scottish mistress. He was far too polite to mention either thing and the evening, far from the disaster of blown cover and guillotined social aspiration I anticipated, went off without a hitch. Everyone had a good time while I grinned, squirmed, and my father assumed the role of host and raconteur, carrying himself as if his present claims had never been in doubt. He was a sportsman, a successful hotel owner, urbanely teasing Janie and flirting with her, sympathizing with Tony over the rigours of medical tuition, quizzing Pete about the theatre and the stockmarket. He grinned, waving for another bottle. He was no enemy of the respect they showed him and when Janie stood up on tiptoe, giving him a kiss, he beamed and spread his arms as if Jack Rayner could hold the world.

Next morning he pulled out a fat wad and handed me five tenners. Another lovely day was in prospect and he and Connie had decided on Newmarket, the races. 'Look after yourself, son,' he said, a little tearful, hugging me tight. 'Keep in touch, eh?' The white Jag whispered away down St Andrew's Street with a wealthy confident sound, my father at the wheel. His right hand was out of the window, and he waved and made a circle, tally-ho!

A few nights after the panic of my father's visit a friend, the actor who'd been the lead in my Joe Orton thing, looked around my rooms and said, 'You don't have any books. Just a few textbooks. How very bizarre. You must be the only person in Cambridge without his shelves stuffed.'

It was as if he'd announced, 'You don't exist,' and yet, as a kid, right up until Cambridge, I'd been so enraptured by books. I'd forgotten until that moment all those nights I'd spent, unable to sleep, with *Wuthering Heights*, P. G. Wodehouse, and Evelyn Waugh. I thought of the Agatha Christie paperbacks I'd collected, with guns and daggers on the covers, or a glass of pink champagne fizzing with cyanide, or a house in the trees where X marked the spot.

I went to Heffer's, the big university bookshop, and signed up for an account. I bought Dryden's *Poems*, a thick red paperback, as well as Nabokov's *The Defence*, and *The Clown* by Heinrich Böll. Inside Heffer's it was like a cave, or rather a network of caves, one book-filled room leading to another, inviting and snug. The smells of ink and paper, the very shelves themselves were a reassuring arm around the shoulder. The future would be fine. In there I was no longer flashing about, but earthed, grounded. I began to go to Heffer's every day, two or three times a day, and then to Cambridge's other bookshops. I haunted those places. I couldn't control myself. It was necessary to possess all sorts of books. The new collection of poems by Robert Lowell. Who could live without a *Gray's Anatomy*? Others might have been able to resist Boswell's *London Journal*, not me. Hugh Thomas's *Spanish Civil War* would more than do, ditto pretty much anything by Raymond Chandler. The fever soon alluded to every genre.

I thought I'd try stealing a book, just one, to see if I still had the nerve. *The Sermons of John Donne* started it, the Cambridge University Press edition, quite plain, with a tan and red dust jacket and handsome black boards. The paper inside was thick and stiff, with the golden colour of Cornish ice-cream. Reading the sermon given at St Paul's, Christmas Day 1621, I tasted bliss: 'If thou canst take this light of reason that is in thee, this poor snuffe, that is almost out in thee, thy faint or dimme knowledge of God, that riseth out of the light of nature, if thou canst in those embers, those cold ashes, find out one small coale, and wilt take the pain to kneell downe, and blow that coale with thy devout *Prayers*, and light thee a *little candle . . .*'

The appearance of this book was simple, beautiful, as I've said; its rhythms promised salvation. I thought I'd found my 'one small coale' and for a week I carried the sermons with me everywhere, the only time that I've had a glimmer of what it might be to have a faith. I didn't dare tell Janie or anyone and when the feeling went out again I was both disappointed and a little glad, because I wasn't sure I knew how to keep the light burning.

I stole a first edition of *Scoop* with the jacket art Waugh did himself, offered for £75 by the Heffer's second-hand and antiquarian department. I stole the sturdy and solemn-looking Yale edition of the works of Samuel Johnson, one volume at a time. Heinemann firsts of *Enderby Outside*, *Tremor of Intent* and *A Clockwork Orange* by Anthony Burgess. The *Collected Poems* of A. E. Housman, Cape 1939, buckram bound. A cased Cassell edition of *The*

Father Brown Stories. Harold Nicolson's biography of George V, A. J. P. Taylor's *English History 1914–1945*. Ian McEwan's *First Love, Last Rites*, *Crash* by J. G. Ballard. I stole books every day. Expeditions were launched first thing in the morning and again late in the afternoon – I wore a baggy jacket and marched out with books tucked in the armpit. The elegant John Murray edition of Byron's correspondence – I stole two at a time, Byron being slimmer than Johnson. Stole the *War Memoirs* of David Lloyd George, brick-heavy, but I thought I'd better give them a whirl. The Neville Spearman first of *A Walk on the Wild Side* by Nelson Algren, daftly under-priced at 25p on one of the stalls in the Market Square. I stole it anyway. I made the acquaintance of Saul Bellow, Norman Mailer, Philip Roth in the shape of various firsts stolen from all over town. Stole first editions of John Stuart Mill's *Autobiography*, *Bleak House* and *Ariel* by Sylvia Plath. *Black Mischief*, another old Chapman & Hall first, no dj, but handsome mottled brown boards. A 1788 three-volume reprint of Johnson's *Rambler* essays, leather bound, black, with gilt lettering. I loved those things. Stole *Webster's Collegiate Thesaurus*. The first *Raymond Chandler Omnibus* (Hamish Hamilton). *Finnegans Wake*. The Penguin P. G. Wodehouse novels, a rare excursion into paperback because I liked the artwork. Nabokov's *Ada*, *Lolita*, and *The Gift* (Paivi was right), as well as the four hardback volumes of his annotated translation of *Eugene Onegin*, boldly boosted in a Routledge boxed set from Bowes & Bowes.

I went mad. My head was a swarm of books. My rooms were full – books on the shelves, on the desk, piles of books on the chairs, books heaped up against the skirting boards.

'But Rich, are you going to read all these?' asked Janie.

I was, I intended to, but that wasn't the point – they were lovely things, magical objects. In Dee Brown's *Bury My Heart At Wounded Knee* I read that in the months before the tribe's final defeat a breakaway sect of Sioux Indians preached that the performance of a ritual known as the ghost dance, followed by the putting on of a magical garment, the ghost shirt, would render them invulnerable. US Cavalry bullets would pass through and leave them unharmed. One evening, at about six, just as Heffer's was about to shut, when assistants were already positioned either side of the glass doors, I walked in and carried out again towards Trinity Street – openly, with no attempt at concealment – the buff-jacketed Harvard edition of W. Jackson Bate's biography of Keats and a white Chapman & Hall omnibus of Evelyn Waugh's 'Sword of Honour' trilogy. As I walked I said under my breath, 'Won't see me, can't see me, won't see me, can't see me.'

One night before we were going out Janie came early to my rooms and said we should spend some time apart. I sat down and wept. I played my last trump and told her the truth about my father, almost all of it – I missed out the bit about him being in gaol.

'He vanished when I was a kid,' I said. 'He only came back last year.'

She reached for my hand. 'Oh, Rich.'

This revelation kept us together for another month or so, but by then the writing was on the wall, in the shape of Stuart, a third-year English undergraduate at Queens'. Stuart had a leather jacket, he wore aviator sunglasses, and he had a motorcycle. He was all asmoulder, and so I got to play another role from my repertoire of adolescent *Sturm und Drang*. Many more tears. I sent flowers and letters. I pleaded with her, with her friends, I phoned her parents. 'Shape up, Rich,' said her mother cheerfully. 'It'll all be topping.' I wrote poems, a short story, about Janie, no, to her. I enlisted the aid of an abscess so the bottom of my face swelled up. I looked like Richard Nixon and a world had ended.

In the Cambridge Market Square there was an old brass fountain, tarnished with age, gummed up with drinking straws and cigarette butts, and always smelling of urine. Drunks lolled and snoozed on its steps, cradling tins of Carlsberg Special Brew or bottles of Anglia Sherry, quite lethal, purchased from any local off-licence for 49p. The story was that one of them was a former don, an eccentric figure with his paunch and wild grey hair, and one of those plaid American hunting caps with flaps at the side. He was always shaking, as if shivering away some attack, or perhaps it was the DTs. Reputedly he'd been a brilliant philosophy lecturer, the protégé of Wittgenstein himself. Now, for the price of a pint, the master's one-time heir would recite the first five pages of the *Tractatus Logico-Philosophicus*.

I believed the story while finding it at the same time utterly unfeasible. I didn't see how anyone could snap and go over the edge. The world was there to be conquered, if you were any good. Failure could be handled, indeed *must* be handled; as Noël Coward had said, success was merely the infinite capacity for dealing with it. I was against moral slipping or any seepage of morale. I didn't believe in leaky boats.

I owed the college £652.75.

It doesn't seem such a huge sum now, nor did it a little while later when my debts rose into the thousands, but it might as well have been a million. One morning there was a letter in my pigeon-hole from the Bursar. It was typed and it said the college would stop me from graduating unless I paid up.

I burst out from within the cloisters, ran through Front Court, ran panting past the duck pond, ran past the stairs where my name was now painted at the bottom, and ran up the four flights to find my bedder Mrs Swiggins waiting on the landing. 'Och, isn't he in a hurry this morning?' she said. 'Lots of revision, no doubt. Lots of work for the wee brain to be getting on with.'

Could they really stop me graduating? Did they have the power? I stuffed the letter to the back of a drawer and tried not to think about it. For the rest of the day I went about business as usual: lectures, lunch, a cards session with Pete afterwards, then a run around the book shops. £652.75 – otherwise I couldn't graduate. I considered going to the Bursar's office, but that idea made me crawl with shame. No, I had to get the money, which meant three options: borrow, earn, or steal. My stepfather was the most likely candidate as far as borrowing was concerned, but I couldn't face explaining to him either. I didn't think of selling my books. I wrote letters to three or four London papers, asking for freelance work. This would take time, I realized, and they might not get back to me at all. I picked up a book to read, *In Hazard*, Richard Hughes' novel of a typhoon at sea, another stolen first. It was almost dark, but people were still playing on the tennis courts below.

I'm left handed. As a child, at one of the schools I went to in Wales, I'd been forced for a number of months to write with my right, with the result that my handwriting has always been a mess. I can make it pretty much whatever I want, and, that evening in Cambridge, as a ball went *poiing* against a racket on the lawns outside my window, I practised my signature, with my left hand, then my right. I had it sloping forwards, elegantly, then back in a cramped awkward style. I made it big and round, I made it a spidery scrawl, and, glancing up into the light of the standard lamp above my desk, I saw what I'd do.

I'd forge cheques.

I was so excited I had to stand up, spin around the room a couple of times, then force myself to sit down. I was breathless. *I'd forge cheques.* I made a quick calculation of how many I'd have to do. Twenty-two. But there'd be expenses – so twenty-five, or even thirty.

I didn't plan to become Al Capone. No one was going

to get hurt. Fraud wasn't so bad and, besides, this was a crime I knew I could do. The essence of the procedure – writing out a cheque – was followed by me quite legally each time I went to the bank, and there was, in the shape of ten thousand or so Cambridge students, an almost limitless supply of cheque-books.

I'd have to go down to London to do this – the activity would be conspicuous here, too few banks. Train fare would be an extra expense, therefore. Say thirty cheques. Say three cheques a day, once I got into the swing. Eleven or twelve days. A little over two weeks' work, that was all.

No, no, I thought, it's too silly.

Most students didn't use their cheque-books often. They kept them in their rooms, which were usually unlocked. I could walk right in – be a breeze.

I did nothing for a couple of days, but whether I was working, or in the bar with the Sex Pistols on the jukebox, or playing cards with Pete and the rest, I was aware of the thought, not unpleasant, a thrilled pressure of the mind. A solution had presented itself. I only had to be bold.

Bank security worked slower then. The system wasn't computerized. You could walk into any bank, it didn't have to be a branch of the one that had issued the cheques, write a cheque, and hand over the guarantee card. It was up to the cashier to compare the signatures. The most cash you could get in one day in this manner was either thirty or fifty pounds, depending on how good a customer you were. Then the cheque went into the system.

I went to my own bank in the Market Square and

watched what the cashier did as I wrote one of my own cheques and handed it in. He barely glanced at the card before turning over the cheque and stamping it.

I put in some more thought. I'd have two clear days. The banks would take at least that long to distribute updated lists of stolen cards, even if the thefts were noticed and reported immediately. And then there was the question of where to make a start. I plumped for Churchill, one of the new colleges, a scattering of white concrete cubes at the northern edge of town. I reasoned that distance would bring safety. Fewer people would recognize me. Besides, the smouldering Stuart, who'd stolen Janie from me, went to Churchill. Might be rather fun to rob him, I thought; that was too crazy, but by then the matter was settled in my mind – Churchill it was.

Everything went so smoothly. It was the dinner hour, and the first room I tried was unlocked and empty. The cheque-book was in the centre drawer of the desk with the guarantee card handily tucked between the stubs and the almost full portion of the book that hadn't been used yet. At the back of the drawer I found a credit card as well.

My new life began.

I put on the blue suit and took the train to London, where I went first of all, not to a bank, but to Harrods', picking out a white silk scarf and paying for it with the stolen credit card. I made my hand stiff and signed the name I'd been practising all the way down: Sandy Wells. It was accepted without a glance, but, in an excess of caution, I dawdled around the other counters, holding my gift-wrapped package as though it were a bomb. Was I being followed? Were store detectives on my trail? 'Oh, come on,' I told myself. I couldn't believe it'd been so easy.

On the steps outside the Sloane Street entrance I made a bargain, that if I counted to twenty and no one came after me it would mean that I'd never be caught doing any of this. Waiting and counting, with my eyes shut, I heard the honking of taxis, the rumble and swish of the revolving doors behind. When I'd got to twenty and no one had come I took out the scarf and draped it around my neck.

Then I almost was caught.

The bank was small, with only one cashier waiting behind the security glass at the counter. The paint was yellow, a little faded, and a poster on the wall said, COME TO FRANCE. I joined the queue, thinking it was all to the good that there were so many people, because the cashier would be pressed – in a hurry. A clock up there told me it was nearly lunchtime. More than an hour had whipped by in Harrods' without my noticing. This was fun.

When at last I got to the front of the queue I realized the cheque-book wasn't in my hand where it should have been, but down at my side, still tucked away in the briefcase. Would look awkward fiddling around to get it out now. No matter – I'd use the card.

'I'd like to get some cash,' I told the cashier, a young woman in her twenties. She wore a white blouse and the skin beneath her neck was freckled and pink, flushed from the heat of the day. I looked up into her eyes, and she looked back, a little longer than I liked, so long I felt uncomfortable.

'Thirty pounds,' I said.

'This'll just take a minute,' she said. She went to the back of the bank and picked up a phone. Had she guessed? I told myself not to be unreasonable. But then the woman in Harrods' hadn't phoned anybody. I smiled at the chap behind me. I smiled at the fellow to the side and when I looked straight back ahead at the counter I was still smiling. I'd have needed a wrench to squeeze away that smile. It was fixed like *rigor mortis*. All at once I realized that the routine involved phoning up for a credit check. Of course! The figure at the bottom of the statement each month that told you how much you could spend. And while there was no chance that a forged cheque would be spotted for at least a day or so, it was very possible that the credit card company knew about the theft of this particular card. The knowledge was one phone call away, from Sandy Wells. Cambridge undergraduates were likely to be efficient about that sort of thing. How did the system work? Were details of theft fed into a computer which printed out lists? If so, how often? Daily – hourly? Was the cashier on the phone to someone, a bespectacled clerk going down a printout with a ruler, waiting to underline me?

I didn't have a clue what I was doing. I was engaged in an activity that involved the risk of capture, trouble, maybe gaol, and I'd done not even the most basic research.

I was sweating, I was faint. The yellow on the walls was brilliant and burning. The wrinkled French peasant clutching his baguette in the poster was leering just at me. No one else seemed to have noticed. They couldn't know. Not possibly, of course not. The flushed cashier was still on the phone.

I picked up my briefcase and walked out. A middle-aged man in a suit gave me a look. There was a rumpus behind me when I reached the door. Someone called out, 'Sir,' but by then I was out into the midsummer blaze of Knightsbridge. Without looking back or thinking I scurried down the steps into the Underground, through the station, up the other side, across the street, down another entrance, then down the escalators and on to the platform as a northbound train rumbled in.

I didn't know how close I'd been to getting caught – it felt like very. But I still had the cheque-book and cheque guarantee card. I passed a sponge over the disaster of the first bank. I thought of the success of Harrods', knowing that unless I went into another bank and made myself I'd never again have the nerve. You had to get back on the horse immediately after falling off, wasn't that the theory? Not that I'd ever fallen off a horse, or even been on one. The train stopped at Covent Garden, Holborn, and at Russell Square I got out, crossing the platform to catch a southbound. Thirty seemed an awful lot of cheques now.

I'd learned a lesson. If I felt anything odd, the merest whisper of being caught, I'd leave. I really didn't want to be caught.

On Bond Street I went into the first bank I saw, joining the queue, writing out the cheque while I waited but only adding the signature when at the counter so the cashier, another young woman who this time I looked straight in the eye, could see. I took care to pause, not for too long, counting the six fivers I'd asked for. I placed them inside my brown leather wallet with the word *Mexico* embossed on the front and only then, with a 'Thanks', another smile at the cashier, did I leave.

With a little glow I walked down through Mayfair to a pub. I fingered the silk scarf around my neck. I saw myself like Pete, not rich, not yet, but dashing. For lunch I had a pint and a packet of Golden Wonder crisps.

Cambridge sweltered through the yearly frenzy known as finals. The college bars were empty until nine or ten at night, then students staggered from their rooms or the libraries to gulp at a desperate pint or several. Some spoke of the two Dickens novels they were reading each day or how they went to sleep at night with tape-recorders spewing out facts of anatomy. There was the story of an undergraduate at St Cat's who couldn't take it any more and hanged himself in his rooms. No one was surprised. Some presented a cooler image, irritating smirks of confidence. 'Oh, that fucking Rayner,' I was amazed to hear someone say. 'He thinks he's in for a first.'

'Hey, Rayner,' Pete said, 'let's make a pact.' Rather than working more, we flaunted our laziness. Rather than slowing down on the drinking we stepped it up, and, having collapsed in a shop doorway opposite King's Chapel, sang 'Desperado' by the Eagles. We took punts in the afternoon or hung out with Charlie, a local kid whose parents owned Belinda's Coffee Bar. Charlie had a green MGB and with the top down we took a spin out to Newmarket, to the races, where we drank white wine, and made large, stupid bets.

An initiative of the previous summer paid dividends. A merchant bank to which I had written on *headed notepaper* now wrote in return, offering an interview. I didn't know what merchant bankers did. I had a sketchy idea of men in back rooms controlling Europe. The profession seemed to hold out the promise of solidity allied to a certain sexy freewheeling capitalism that might be just the niche for my talents. I was sure I had some. The letter said there were six candidates for two jobs. The interview would take place, not in the offices of the bank (it was Crédit Suisse) or a hotel room, but over dinner at L'Epicure, a swanky restaurant outside Cambridge.

They'd taken a private room. The candlelit table was set with ten places, which meant the six candidates, all male, and four people from the bank, all men as well. I wore the blue suit.

Champagne was followed by Meursault was followed by Chateauneuf-du-Pape. *Foie gras* was followed by trick food, by salmon and duck. A bank guy with glasses sought my opinion about the England cricket team. A bank guy without glasses, seeing me reach for a frog's leg, asked how I felt about foreign travel.

'Oh, I love it,' I said, crunching down a mouthful of bone. 'My father's a diplomat. In Australia.' I was quite gleeful, uncaring whether the bluff was called or not. No, I admitted, he hadn't yet reached ambassadorial rank.

One of the candidates I knew: Mark Greaves, from Magdalene – charming, and he'd got firsts all the way. Mature beyond his years, fleshy, a little balding, he already looked the part. A shoo-in. Another was a research student from Trinity, nervy, but with the composure to drink and say as little as possible. The competition.

Everything was going pretty well, from the point of view of my merchant banking future, until, while we were waiting for dessert, Mark told a joke and then glanced across the table, challenging me to tell one too. There was a brief volley of joke telling and I remember thinking that this had better stop now. I looked around the table, at the watchful bankers, the quietly eager guy from Trinity, cheeks gleaming. I plunged, riffing on a sketch I'd written about a dippy doctor who steals his patients' shoes. Dessert came and went. Mark recited Edward Lear. I countered with 'The Walrus and the Carpenter'. There was more champagne, brandies, cigars. He told a story about Polish virgins. I remembered a typically doomy one of Fred's, the gardener at the Old Manor, concerning a deaf railway engineer who had his head knocked clean off by an Intercity 125. After the dinner was over, when I was waiting for a taxi back to the town, one of the bankers came up to me in the lobby.

'Very entertaining,' he said, languidly assured, smelling of brandy and cigars. 'Good luck.'

'Thanks,' I said, and circled my hand in the air. 'Tally-ho!' Sometimes I did worry – what if I were my father's copy? I didn't believe so, though I didn't know what I was.

The Mexico wallet had been given to me by my mother, who'd had it from my stepfather, who'd bought it during his travels as an officer in the merchant navy during WW II. It went with me on my trips to London, for which I'd by then developed rituals, my own little rumba. The blue suit was kept carefully folded along with the cheque-books and the white silk scarf in a bag in one of the left-luggage lockers at Cambridge station. I didn't want to leave Emmanuel each morning dressed up like a peacock. I made sure that I got to the station in good time and changed there. All the ticket collectors came to know me. Some nodded or said hello. One had buck teeth and a shrill voice, high as a castrato. First he regarded my daily transformation with suspicion, then a wondering silence. At last he said, 'Are you a comedian?'

I'd checked what time dinner happened in each college and went on my expeditions then. Rooms were usually empty, but in case they weren't I had a roll of Salvador Dali posters to offer for sale. I only had reason to resort to this a couple of times. I always knocked on the door three times, three times for luck, knock on wood. I'd made the bargain outside Harrods', about counting to twenty, which in theory should have taken care of everything in the superstition department, but it seemed as well to be on the safe side. Sometimes I had to search a bit further than the desk. Once I looked in a wardrobe and was surprised to find a rack of dresses. I was in a girl's room. I had a sudden flutter of panic and guilt.

I believed in the magic of my own nerve, that it was a shield, a force to keep others away and myself safe. I became quite blasé, almost bored. I got a thrill selling a dripping Dali clock to a bearded biochemistry student having robbed the room next door. Trancelike in London I went from bank to bank and jumped one morning when a cashier said quite casually: 'Would you mind signing this again? Just do it on the back.'

I knew that I was going to be caught and sent to gaol. I'd end up like the philosopher in the Market Square, if I was lucky. I blinked and for a few moments was a tree struck by lightning, shivering off its bark.

I told myself to be very calm. Though I was concentrating on signing the cheque – not too slow, Christ you're taking for ever, *don't muff this* – I was aware all the while of his eyes, which moved from my hand, to my face, and back to my hands again. When I pushed the cheque back through the grille he stared at me quite openly. I was sure he knew. He compared the signatures again, holding the cheque between two fingers in both hands, and leaning down to squint at the guarantee card. 'How would you like the money, sir?'

Most of the time it all went without a hitch. I'd say something after the cashier had checked the signature, hoping to deflect his or her attention for a second so the date wouldn't get ticked off in the calendar box at the back and I'd be able to use the same book again that day.

British Rail shuttled me from Cambridge to Liverpool Street and back and forth between two modes of thinking. Somewhere along the line the switch was thrown. I had to be convincing at this game. I was the young businessman in his blue suit. I'd only just started but I was eager and on the way up, confident of my accounts. I'd indicate with a smile that I was in a bit of a hurry. In the parks at lunchtime I was still in character. If someone started a conversation I told them I was a trainee lawyer with the firm that had fired me the previous summer. I happily gave out the firm's phone number. 'Phone me some time and we'll have a drink.'

London grew hotter by the day. Between one and two thirty the parks were packed. Office boys changed into shorts, set up stumps and played cricket. Barristers in striped trousers went boating on the Serpentine or snoozed beneath tents of *The Times*. A secretary kicked off her shoes and stepped out of her dress revealing a bikini beneath. I'd dreamed of such summers. London was going Mediterranean on me again.

By then I should have reached my goal. Except that I'd started spending the money, on booze, clothes, and records, on suits, three velvet suits: one black, one brown, the third deep bottle green like the one Pete had bought the night we went to the Ritz. I'd never been so flush. I took taxis and developed a taste for restaurants. I swanned about Emmanuel in my new plumage and for weeks did no laundry, throwing socks, underwear, and shirts on to a daily growing heap. I bought everything new. Finals came and went, a minor interruption to the routine. When the letter came from the merchant bank, saying I hadn't got the job, that was no bother either. I simply ceased to concern myself with back rooms and Europe. I went to the King's Road, and, after a fruitful morning in the banks, spent £165 on a pair of Chelsea boots, so pointy and tight I knew as soon as I got out of the shop that I'd never really be able to wear them, despite the fact that they'd looked so great in the mirror, those stacked Cuban heels.

When I gave them to Pete they fitted him as if custom made. 'Nice boots,' he said, stroking his Zapata moustache.

From Tony's room I took a white shirt and when, a few days later, he asked if I had, I said no, of course not. In some way I thought I was being accused of theft, of all the theft. Tony came back and heaved the shirt out of my laundry pile. For once the smile was absent from his face. 'What's going on with you?' he said. I could find nothing to say.

That same morning I was browsing in a book in Heffer's when I saw the word 'migraine'. I quickly turned the page, too late. By the time I got out on to Trinity Street I was already in what doctors called 'the haze'. A current seemed to be tingling out of my eyes and skin. My feet felt as though they'd been removed from my shoes and replaced with something – cotton wool, steel wool, some fibre – that was rubbing raw the nerves in the ends of my legs. A chair in the window of Belinda's coffee bar tried to hook my eye and pop it out of my head, which was no longer aching, but sizzling with pain. I vomited in the wash basin as soon as I made it up the stairs to my rooms. I went on vomiting, hour after hour. This was the worst attack in years, and when at last the headache went away enough for the Migril, my prescribed drug, to send me to sleep for nearly eighteen hours, I didn't dream or stir.

The doctors say that such attacks are connected to extremes of both stress and relaxation, moments when the self is feeling fuzzy. They are warnings. But when I finally woke up my mind felt refreshed – scrubbed clean – and I was ready to go.

It was another hot summer night, and Harry Johnston, a friend from Downing, just down the road from Emmanuel, had come round to see a movie with a gang of us. Harry Johnston was Glaswegian, with tight, curly hair. He wore purple jeans and a black leather German army topcoat, a trophy of his father's from WWII, and an item he carried with him at all times, even in this, one of the hottest summers of the century. He always had more money than the rest of us, Pete included. He was a drug dealer, everyone knew. The idea occurred to me when I saw him put the key to his rooms in his coat and leave the coat on a chair at Pete's place.

The Sentinel was a horror film in which an old man, played by Burgess Meredith, stood guard over the entrance to hell on earth. This, according to the story, had been someone's job since the expulsion of Satan and his cohorts from heaven; it got passed down from generation to generation, like land, or membership of the Marylebone Cricket Club. The underworld's gateway was located behind a mirror in the otherwise sparsely furnished living-room of an apartment in New York's Greenwich Village.

I told Pete I had to take a leak, left the cinema, went back to Emmanuel, found the key in the pocket of the leather coat, and went down the street to Downing. At dusk, walking through the sandstone glow of the wide and spacious Front Court, I was calm and purposeful, planning a really big score. In Harry Johnston's rooms I was sure there'd be cash. If I found heroin or marijuana I'd sell it.

There were no drugs, Harry Johnston was too smart for that, but there was cash (some, nothing like the bundle I'd hoped for), a cheque-book, a credit card, and a Rolex watch. I stowed all this in a canvas bag that on the way out I slid beneath a bush at the entrance to the Master's Lodge, knowing I'd pick it up later. Then it was a quick sprint to Emmanuel to return the key and I was back in the cinema before the oogie-boogies had even started coming up from hell yet.

The next morning Harry Johnston sat in the same chair in Pete's room, sunglasses on, leather coat beside him in a forlorn heap. He told the story of how he'd been ripped off. Officers from the Flying Squad had been poking around until the wee hours, he said.

I heard this in a melting swoon. I'd thought that because

he was a drug dealer he wouldn't dare to call the cops. Wasn't that the way it was supposed to work, since he was a bad guy himself? And the Flying Squad! They were the élite, the crack force of the British police, with powers to move outside conventional boundaries and behave pretty much as they pleased. The image had been created by a long-running TV show, *The Sweeney* (Cockney rhyming slang: Sweeney Todd, Flying Squad), in which the actors John Thaw and Dennis Waterman dressed in suits not dissimilar to my blue one, uttered obscenities, and screeched about in souped-up Ford Granadas, behaving all in all like a combination of Sherlock Holmes and Jimmy Cagney. Now they were looking for me.

'They said one of my friends probably did it,' Harry Johnston said, swinging a foot with a Texan boot on the end of it. 'They wanted a list – I told them none of my friends would do something like that. I didn't want them bothering you all.'

A drug dealer, outraged that he'd been robbed, none the less refused to give up the names of his friends – but then I knew he had his own good reasons for not wanting the Flying Squad to poke too deeply.

Harry Johnston. I can hardly say the name. The last I heard of him was when the Downing magazine asked what old alumni were up to and he sent back the reply: 'Pimp at the Tai-Pei Hilton.' I'm ashamed – Harry Johnston had been a friend. I feel the same dizzy weightlessness I did then, my mouth suddenly dry as he said: 'I've got some friends coming from London. Business associates. They've put the word out to places where this bastard might try to sell my cameras. We're going to do a little investigation of our own.' He grinned, showing sharp teeth under those all-reflecting sunglasses. 'If we find him, we'll kill him.'

The IRA launched a campaign to disrupt the Queen's Silver Jubilee, the twenty-fifth anniversary of her rule. A bomb went off at King's Cross railway station. Another exploded near St Paul's Cathedral. There were few casualties, but London, already stiflingly hot, was in chaos.

I was glad I'd been in the room when Harry Johnston made his threat, so now at least I knew to wait for a while before trying to offload the Rolex and all the other stuff I'd retrieved from beneath the rhododendrons at Downing. I went right ahead with his credit card and cheque-book, however, working the banks in the City when I came into Liverpool Street and found that the Underground into the West End was shut because of a bomb scare at Oxford Circus. It was after midday before I arrived in my more usual haunts. With plenty of cash in my pocket I thought I deserved a treat: Simpson's – rare roast beef, a bottle of claret. Smiling at an attractive American tourist, I did for a moment fancy myself a dashing fictional character: Raffles as played by David Niven, amateur cracksman, exceptional crook and perhaps the very finest sportsman of his generation.

Afterwards, drunk, I sauntered along Piccadilly, and stepped for a moment inside the Wren church, set back from the street, cool and spacious. After that I went into a very grand bank, with columns and a marble floor, and let routine take over, my hand quite steady as I wrote the cheque.

On the train back to Cambridge I realized I didn't have my briefcase. My hand flew on to the seat beside me, my eyes scanned the luggage racks, though I knew I wouldn't find it there; I'd left it in the bank, on top of the counter, shut but unlocked. There was a book in it, together with the pad on which I'd practised the signatures, and – what else? I tried to think. British Rail cushions exuded the smell of ancient dust. Sometimes I kept my own bank statements in a flap at the back of the case. If the bank spotted the passing of that particular forged cheque, found the briefcase, the pad with the signatures, and if I had left one or more of my own bank statements – well. Most considerate of you, Mr Raffles, to leave a calling card. I pictured capture, arrest, trial. I pictured trying to explain this to my mother. Oh God.

The very finest sportsman of his generation was sick in the train lavatory.

I really didn't want to get caught. So why then had I left the briefcase? It was just a mistake, perhaps, but a mistake made during an activity where a high price might be paid for bad breaks, where hitches might easily lose their usual quality of correctability and come to seem fateful. Now, more than ever, I needed a hefty slice of luck and on the walk back from Cambridge station I touched every piece of wood I saw, leaping from one to the other, and simultaneously counting to nine, twenty-seven, seventy-one, no, had to be *eighty*-one, not even knowing why I believed multiples of three brought good luck. The Father, the Son, and the Holy Ghost?

At this rate it was going to take me all night to get back to college – I made another of my bargains. I reminded myself that there was no way the bank could know yet that I'd forged Harry Johnston's cheque. All they had was the briefcase, and therefore what I had to do was clear. I had to go and get it back; if I did that, and I was successful, I'd get away with the Harry Johnston thing as well. He and his friends would never catch up with me. That seemed fair.

Next day I was back at the bank within a minute or so of opening. Two other customers were already inside, and there was a uniformed police officer, standing to one side beneath the high windows. I had a few horrible seconds before I realized he was there in case of terrorists, not a Cambridge student with fraudulent tendencies. I wasn't sure what this single plump and benign-looking bobby would be able to do against two or three IRA fellows armed with automatic weapons, but no matter. Most likely everyone else was pleased to see him.

The cashier was a woman, with fairish hair cut strict around her face. She looked at me sharply when I mentioned that I rather thought I'd left my briefcase in the bank the previous day.

'I'll get the manager.'

I paced the marble floor, grinning, telling myself they

can't know, they can't know. An oak door at the side opened and the manager popped out, an eager balding fellow in blue pinstripe. He pranced forward with my briefcase in both hands like an offering.

'You gave us quite a fright.'

'Sorry about that.'

'We had to evacuate the bank. That was after we'd called the Bomb Squad.'

'The Bomb Squad?' I said, voice rising. 'No, really?'

This was the policeman's cue to step forward. 'This *is* your briefcase, sir.'

'That's right.'

'Then perhaps you'd like to tell me what was inside, if you don't mind, sir.'

I was in a bit of a fog. I said there'd been a notepad.

'Yes, we wondered about that. Found it a little . . . odd,' said the policeman. 'The signatures and all.'

'I doodle,' I said, trying to sound offhand. 'On the train.'

'That's all right, sir,' he said. 'People will have their foibles. And was there anything else you can think of, in the briefcase, I mean?'

'Oh well, yes,' I said. 'Of course there was a book.' There was always a book. There *is* always a book. Socks can be odd, but the book that is to be a travelling companion, that has to be perfect.

'And what book might that have been?' said the policeman.

'It was by Flann O'Brien. A hardback. A first edition of

the second novel he wrote, not published until 1967, after his death.'

'Yes, sir,' said the policeman, round red face all friendliness now. 'We noticed that it was a nice book. And what might the title of the novel have been, that's if you don't mind me asking?'

'It was *The Third Policeman*.'

'A little alarming, sir, I don't mind telling you, giving everyone a scare like that.' My policeman, my first policeman – there were to be others – rocked to and fro on squeaky Doc Marten soles. '*Very* alarming.'

'Yes,' I said, 'I can see that. I'm really most terribly sorry.'

'The fellows from the Bomb Squad, and the lads back at the station, well . . .' He drew out a big white handkerchief and more or less stuffed it in his mouth, trying very hard to maintain an air of appropriate dignity. 'I don't know that I've ever seen anyone laugh so hard.'

The Queen's Silver Jubilee took place, despite the bombs, and Pete, Tony and I met up at 10 a.m. in the cobbled courtyard of the Eagle. We got drunk, as did the whole of Cambridge that day. At some point during the afternoon I ripped my trousers and changed into the rented tuxedo I'd be wearing that night when we planned to crash the Clare May Ball. In the event, we approached the college porter, a bowler-hatted figure of plump and almost priestly authority, and bribed him. He issued us with the little orange discs that said we were bullet proof.

Once inside, Pete was very much the *flâneur* in his suit of bottle-green velvet. Tony, defiantly uncool, was drunk in the most extravagant way, clad only in a pair of microscopic red swimming briefs, and set out his stall at the bar. I competed by signing for seven or eight bottles of champagne under the name Rev. Raymond Hockley, who happened to be the chaplain of our own college. I saw Janie there, with the smouldering Stuart, which was embarrassing, and, by an odd chance, the same punk I'd met the year before, the one who'd said, 'Six vodkas and limes, which is what Oi've just 'ad.' Billy Idol, as it turned out, whose band Generation X was playing at the ball that night.

Eventually Pete and I were rumbled. Five beefy Boat club types came up and demanded to know which of us was the Rev. Raymond Hockley. We had to make a run for it, across the bridge, between the torches which flickered and hissed on the path beside the Fellows' Garden. Tony was safe at the bar somewhere, but with the noise of Generation X thumping behind, and the goons in pursuit, Pete and I scrambled up the high steel gate at the back of the college.

I paused for a moment at the top, fifteen, maybe twenty feet off the ground. The river gave off an earthy summer smell – mushrooms in a bag. Soon I'd be walking back through the town in the light of dawn, kicking my heels on a misty summer morning. Cambridge was over, and I promised myself I'd never have anything to do with crime again – no more magic orange discs, no more ghost shirts. Ahead were trees and shadows, a road, the ominous bulk of the University Library.

I jumped down to the other side.

Six

Weeks sweltered by. I sat in the garden rereading the first four cantos of *Don Juan*. My mother and stepfather were in the kitchen, peeping at me over their papers. 'What do you expect?' I heard my stepfather say through the window. 'He's just a loafer.'

Pete had gone to work for his father, as an executive with a big food corporation, the one that owned the company that owned the company that made Golden Wonder potato crisps. Tony was at medical school and meanwhile I mooned about. From a local bookshop I stole a first edition of Eliot's *The Four Quartets*. I returned for a lovely Collins first of *Byron: The Years of Fame* by Peter Quennell.

Wimbledon was another drug, though I missed the final where Borg came back from 1–4 in the final set to beat Connors. I was in London at an old school friend's wedding. Fortunately he was a tennis nut. At the reception he sat, like a king, still in his top hat in the centre of the room, granting audience and twiddling with a transistor radio. Shouts went up of, 'It's the Swede, the Swede.' Later when he asked me what I was up to I said I was writing. 'Oh, that's the life,' he said.

I'd given up on my Cambridge novel. I was trying my hand at another. I bought notebooks and plenty of sharp new pencils. I recorded the opening of 'Burnt Norton' from *The Four Quartets* in my own voice and played it back to myself each night over the stereo in my bedroom.

> Time present and time past
> Are both perhaps present in time future,
> And time future contained in time past.
> If all time is eternally present
> All time is unredeemable.'

I made day trips to Ilkley, Leeds, Bradford, and York. In the trains I moved from carriage to carriage, unable to settle for long. When my stepsister came to stay at the Old Manor I stretched out in front of the TV and watched golf while she and Denise Robinson, one of her pretty friends, talked about a party. 'It's in the Lake District,' said my stepsister. 'It's going to be absolutely *wonderful*.'

Denise Robinson, besides being attractive, came from a rich family; they lived up on The Grove, a private road opposite the Old Manor. 'There'll be no prob getting the car,' she said. 'Mummy and Daddy are away.' Mummy and Daddy were summering on a Greek island, or Mallorca, the Costa del . . . somewhere. 'We'll leave first thing on Saturday.'

As Tom Watson holed out from the sand with a

miraculous nine-iron swish my idea soared up out of the blue: the Robinsons' house would be empty all weekend – I would rob the Robinsons. As soon as I had the thought I realized I had no choice. I would have to rob them. I was delighted, afraid. I let go with a cheer.

My stepsister sniffed. 'You're so childish.'

In the family I was famous for being light on my feet. I fancied myself like Disraeli, no true Englishman because he was capable of treading so softly. I practised going soundlessly up the stairs and down them again. I laid out my costume on the bed: dark jeans, black T-shirt, a pair of Adidas trainers. From the attic I pulled down a pair of beige canvas grip bags, covered with dust, and soaped and wiped them clean. From a drawer in my mother's dressing table I took a pair of thin black leather gloves. They were a tight fit and smelled faintly of perfume. I sneaked about while the others were downstairs. I was anxious to get on, do the job right. I couldn't wait for Saturday. Sometimes another voice would pipe up, saying this was stupid and dangerous. I reminded myself of the promise I'd made that night of the Clare May Ball, perched on top of the gate.

I walked up The Grove to case out the Robinsons' place. It was built in blackened Yorkshire sandstone, a big square house with white shutters. Red and green ivy crept up the left side, and an immaculate lawn rolled away from the house down to tall stone gateposts with stone dragons on top, wings outstretched. The house and grounds stood back behind a line of sheltering elms. The house looked solid and prosperous. It looked as though there were treasures inside.

I went back that night for a sense of how it would be in the dark. There were few street lamps on The Grove and, in the middle of one hundred-yard stretch – where trees on either side leaned towards each other, meeting in the middle to form a canopy – it was entirely black, the entrance to a rabbit hole. I could hear my feet, but not see them. I stood quite still for a few seconds, aware of night smells, roses, lavender, and the whisper of foliage overhead. A bat brushed against my face – another touched my arm, a sudden bump. So much for their radar.

'You seem perky,' my mother said.

'I'm in a zone,' I said, 'like Bjorn Borg.'

I sat in the living room with *Don Juan*. Juan had met Julia, 'charming, chaste and twenty-three'. He grew pensive and thought 'unutterable thoughts'. She responded and her husband, Don Alfonso, justly suspicious, searched every nook and cranny of the bedroom, except under the bedclothes where Juan lay hiding, all but suffocated between Julia's legs – until his tell-tale pair of shoes gave him away. While Alfonso went for his sword Juan had to fly! Down the back stairs – handy.

I thought of Denise Robinson who, as she'd left the Old Manor, had turned and given me a little smile. She was the kind of girl I wished to fall in love with. What if she were to be in the house, waiting, when I robbed it? In bed that night I was tucked up with some unutterable thoughts of my own.

But when Saturday came around, there was a problem. My mother and stepfather announced that they weren't going out.

'But you *always* go out on a Saturday night,' I told them.

'Not tonight,' my mother said, obviously in a foul mood.

I slumped in front of the TV. I tried to concentrate on the disc-jockey who was hosting his weekly TV show with a dreadful squirrelly bounciness. I pouted and sulked. I sighed. It wasn't until I'd thrown what amounted to a full-scale tantrum, turning red in the face and announcing well, this said it all – I was never allowed any time to myself in this house – that my mother gave in.

Smiling, I kissed her on the cheek. I helped my stepfather on with his coat and more or less pushed them out of the house. I stood in the road, waving, until the red tail-lights of the Rover had quite disappeared. In minutes I was in costume. I had the two canvas bags, one folded inside the other, along with a torch, some old newspapers, and a roll of inch-wide Sellotape. I walked up The Grove, through the rabbit hole, between the stone gates with the threatening statuary. I was breathing hard. I was a little curious: of course, it was fated, *written*, but was I really going to go through with this? I went around the side of the house and tried the back door, just in case – locked. No matter: I had a plan. I'd stick to my plan. The shadows were thick and warm, friendly.

I hadn't counted on the flower-beds – wide flower-beds, thick with rose bushes. Lovely to sniff, not so easy to wade among with the canvas bags held high above my head. And when at last I did reach the window I'd targeted I found that the stone sill was much higher than appeared from the road. It was level with my heart, so I had to balance the canvas bag on it and hoist myself up after, taking care not to knock the bag off. I stood there a while, side on, pressed against the windowpane, one foot in front of the other as if I were on a tightrope. I felt exposed, not to mention stupid and very frightened, on the one hand in danger of taking a nose-dive into the bushes, on the other quite likely to press too hard on the glass and tumble through that way.

I reached into the bag for the Sellotape, ripped off a few strips with my teeth, criss-crossed the window, then smashed the glass with the end of the torch. I'd seen a burglar do this on the TV. Surprisingly it worked – but then, why not? The glass came away with a sound like crunching sugar.

Found the latch, raised the sash, slid over, pulling the bag after me. Suddenly I was inside.

There was an impression of silence, of space, of a thick pressing darkness that – even though pierced by me a moment before – was already settling back all around. Somewhere there was the tick of a clock, counting time at a much slower beat than once a second. Or so it seemed. Everything was different, as if I were in Captain Nemo's vessel and this the floor at the bottom of the sea. I felt the empty house with my nerve ends: old stone surrounding an atmosphere that asked, politely, that I disrupt it as little as possible, even if I was a thief. The house felt alive, not unwelcoming.

After a few minutes or so my eyes grew accustomed to the darkness. I sensed the proportions of the room I was in. It seemed big, an open area, with width on either side of me and dark patches, doorways I imagined, leading to other rooms beyond.

I turned on the torch. Its beam discovered a fireplace and a mantelpiece with a glinting carriage clock and decorative doodads on top. A mirror flashed light back at me and as I moved the torch those objects vanished while new ones came up out of the darkness. A little round coffee table with dimpled edges. A three-piece suite. To my left, as I'd thought, there was another room, disappearing around a corner. The torch created one half of a dining table and the ribbed backs of two or three chairs. A floor lamp sprang up, with a tasselled shade. I turned off the torch and waited again. Everything had a glow, as if the objects themselves were a source of light, not just reflecting the little that came from outside through the opened curtains. There was no moon.

The carpet was thick and springy, it had bounce, like Denise Robinson's hair. I took down the carriage clock, the doodads, and wrapped them in sheets of newspaper so they wouldn't break when I put them in the bag. I hadn't thought at all about *what* I was going to steal. A house such as this contained a near infinity of objects. Which were valuable and which not? Moving through to the dining-room it was the shiny silver things – candlesticks, a cigarette box, a fruit dish – that caught my attention. I was a hero, stumbling on a dragon's hoard. I was a dumb trout, tempted by the hook.

I moved, making my feet quiet, stealing with an almost

tender care, and from the dining room went into a much thicker darkness where I had to turn on the torch again. This was the hallway, high, with a wood parquet floor and wood panels all around. A staircase was on my left, wide with a carpet, leading up. Light gleamed from glass in picture frames. There was a double window with stained glass on the landing.

I left behind the one bag I'd filled and took the stairs two at a time, swinging myself around on the banister at the landing. I was upstairs. A door was open to the right. With the torch on I went quickly in.

This was a bedroom, the master bedroom, where Mr and Mrs Robinson slept. There was a double bed with a plain walnut headboard. There was a tall chest of drawers and a dressing table above which a mirror bounced back light. Most of all there was a confusion of smells: of make-up and perfume, of Brylcreem, of mothballs and musty clothes, of sleep. The curtains were drawn, the carpet thick and soft – the whole impression was cosy, old fashioned, as of a nest lived in by people much older than myself. I'd been in this room a hundred times before – it was my mother and stepfather's.

I swept up the silver dressing table set. There was a case of jewels, heavy and full, on top of the chest of drawers. That went straight into the bag. Sitting on a lace doily there was another case, decorated with mother-of-pearl. Inside were rings, ear-rings, chains and brooches all caught together, a knot of treasure.

I went back out on to the landing and turned into

another room, also on the right. This one was neat and neutral smelling – the guest room. The curtains were open and I was careful about not letting the beam of the torch strike the darkened windowpanes. Here I am, I thought, I'm a burglar, being a burglar.

Across the landing was a room like my own – a boy's room. Clothes were heaped on a chair. Socks were strewn on the floor, the faces of Bremner, Giles, Charlton and the other members of the Leeds United team of the 1970s looked down from the wall. There was a collection of tarnished Victorian pennies. He kept his in a saucer; at home mine were piled in a tubular red container that had once held laxative for my grandfather.

The next room was that of Denise Robinson herself and I thought I might like to stay in there for ever. The fragrances here were lighter, more delicate, and the room seemed airier. A window was open a few inches at the bottom, letting in a breeze and odours from the night. The bed was made. A teddy bear and hand-stitched cushions were on one side of it, pushed up against a wall. There was a bookshelf with lots of the same books my stepsister had: *Jane Eyre*, *Gone With The Wind*, two or three by R. F. Delderfield, *Rogue Herries* by Hugh Walpole. There was another jewellery case and, on a table, a vase, shapely, made from glass that was opaque and grainy when I touched it. I pressed my lips against Denise Robinson's pillow.

I didn't know how long I'd been in there. I'd lost all track of time. I had to fight against this feeling, the wonderful strangeness of being in a place so familiar in some ways, so like home, and yet utterly strange, as if I'd walked straight into a fairy-tale. I had to be professional. I'd started out well enough downstairs but up here, in the bedrooms, I'd been thrown.

On the way down winking glass caught my attention. I turned the torch.

The picture, huge, was in a gilt frame above the landing. It was of a stag, side on, attention caught – his glance came straight at me. Antlers forked upwards to the top of the frame. In the background there was a river, there were dense misty woodlands, and, behind all, a snow-capped mountain range – the stag, not man, as proud sovereign.

It was a Landseer, not an original, at least I didn't think so, although it might have been for all I knew or know, but a copy in oils old enough to be worth something. In my excitement I ran down the stairs and left the second bag alongside the first and put the torch on top. Then I went back up again and stood beneath the picture. With my arms stretched out wide I could just take the frame at its sides – good. I stood up on tiptoe and lifted, trying to get the picture of its hooks – didn't work. I took a deep breath and tried again, really heaving, a mistake because this time the picture did come away, all of a sudden, and it was so much heavier than expected that I was sent reeling, staggering back. I hit something, the banister, which creaked, groaned, and seemed for a moment sure to break, sending me down fifteen or so feet into the hallway with the picture on top of me, in which position I imagined myself being found by the returning Robinsons, thief crushed by Landseer.

The banister held. Before I had time to congratulate

myself about this the edge of the frame slid through my hands and came down on the stairs with a thump that reverberated and shook throughout the house. I was forced to jump forward quickly so the frame didn't fall and slide away down the stairs. At last I had it steady and I stood there, sweating, panting.

Now I'd really got the bit between my teeth. I saw what the problem was: the frame. It had been absurd to try and take the picture still inside the frame. Struggling down The Grove with that great thing – impossible. And conspicuous? Not much. I had to get the canvas out of the frame and roll it up carefully, the way I'd seen Kirk Douglas in that movie about Vincent Van Gogh. *Lust for Life.*

The painting itself was the valuable thing, correct?

I laid the picture flat on the landing. I nipped back down for the torch and a silver knife I'd taken from the dining-room. I imagined that I'd be able to cut out the canvas from the back, but once I got the frame turned over I realized the impossibility of that idea. This wasn't made like the posters I'd sold at Cambridge, but was solid, secured by wood and extra layers of canvas as well as masking tape, a more recent addition. There were scrawled auction marks in chalk and the name and address of a framer's in Leeds. A date at the top, 1892, alongside which the knife merely added a few ineffectual scratches.

I turned the picture over again. The stag gazed at me with a curious eye. I brought down the end of the torch and cracked the glass, my idea being now to remove the glass and get the canvas out from the front, but when I stood the frame up on its edge and jiggled, expecting the glass to fall away, nothing happened. I gave the glass another whack, a really good one this time with the torch. A piece of glass the size of my thumb-nail plopped out on to the carpet.

I took off my gloves. I ran my hands over the surface of the glass – uneven now, with lots of sharp edges – and attacked the splinters, pulling them out one by one. Somehow I contrived not to cut myself and when I'd cleared away a small area of canvas I put my gloves on again, easing loose the jagged pieces of glass, tugging them away. It was slow going and I'd been at it a little while when something slid inside my concentration, a sound. I hadn't noticed it before. I laid the picture carefully down and stepped down the stairs. I stood spinning in the vastness of the hall, listening, trying to locate the source. It wasn't a ringing, more of a suppressed buzzing, as if someone were trying to shut up a phone, smothering it with a cushion.

I'd assumed all along, before breaking in, that the Robinsons would have an alarm, but, since it hadn't gone off when I'd smashed the window and came in, I'd pushed the thought away, supposing either that they didn't have one after all, or that it had been circumvented by my sheer burglarly skill. I hadn't considered the possibility that there would be an alarm but that it wouldn't go off at first, that there would be a *delay*.

I asked myself why would anyone do that, install an alarm with a delay? Obviously the thing had been tripped the moment I'd broken in, so why hadn't it started ringing then? Because, I realized, the alarm was connected to the police station, and it had been ringing there for a while already.

My head itched. Cold sweat ran down my flesh. My hands were damp, my armpits clammy. In less time than it takes to tell this I went liquid. My insides too: fear, anger at myself for not having seen the possibility, even a little outrage at the deceit, the fact that someone had worked out a trap – all these were sloshing about. I could see every line on the parquet floor. I wished I could make my escape by sinking down into them.

The light filtering through the stained-glass windows on the landing seemed much brighter. Was that the beam of a police car? At that moment the muted buzzing stopped. There was a brief and eerie silence before the alarm started going off full blast. It clanked and thundered. It quivered through the floor with a force designed to make any intruder flee, to force him to get into his car and speed the only way he could, down The Grove, where he'd meet the police coming up the other way.

I didn't have a car. I didn't panic. In a moment I saw what I had to do. I collected the two bags, the torch, all my things, and went to the front door. I had to put down the bags while I fiddled with bolts and locks. But soon I was back out into the night, trotting down the path as fast as I dared with the two bags dragging at my arms. The night was warm and muggy, and still no moon. Here outside the deafening clank of the alarm seemed muted again. What with the big lawns and gardens, and the trees surrounding them, there was a chance the neighbours might not even have heard it. At least that was a plus.

I got to the gates where the dragons stood guard and, instead of turning left down The Grove, I turned in the opposite direction, walking up the hill for a hundred yards or so. I climbed a flimsy wire fence into a field and pulled the bags through after. Far below, at the bottom of the valley, lines of car headlights meandered along beside the river. Above those were the lit-up houses of the council estate I'd helped rebuild. I knew a place to hide the bags. Then I'd walk up the hill back to the Old Manor, maybe even stop for a pint on the way. Between me and where I had to get to was an area perhaps half a mile wide. During the day there was a herd of Jersey cows chewing away. But at night? I saw nothing. In the distance I heard sirens. I walked down into the pitch dark.

'Guess what?' my stepsister said, a little out of breath. She was back from the party in the Lake District. 'The Robinsons were burgled at the weekend.' We were eating breakfast. I had marmaladed toast in one paw and my nose in the sports pages of the *Daily Telegraph*. All that summer the West Indies were handing England another pasting.

'The house was ransacked,' she said.

My stepfather looked up from his own newspaper. 'Disgraceful,' he said.

I took another bite. This was unfair: the house had not

been ransacked. I'd been very careful about that, until the Landseer.

'They got away with amazing stuff,' she said. The Flying Squad had been there most of the day and all of the previous night after Denise had got back. They'd collected evidence and dusted the house for prints. According to them, the 'job' was one of a series that had been 'pulled' in the area.

The Flying Squad had been called in on my account again. I stared at my stepsister and reached for more toast. I'd always found her sexy, though right then I mostly felt smug and superior. You think you know who I am, I thought, but I know better – by day that loafer with the Cambridge degree, but come the night . . . Zorro.

Meanwhile my mother and stepfather worked themselves up into a general litany about lawlessness and society going to the dogs. Granny Michie was called so she could join in too. She recommended the bringing back of the birch. 'It's a terrible, terrible thing,' my stepfather said.

I swelled inside with a daft glory, insanely pleased that my work had been mistaken for that of a professional. I spread marmalade on another luxuriantly buttered piece of toast.

It was only when I was in my own room that something else my stepsister had said sunk in. The Flying Squad had taken fingerprints. All at once I had a clear memory of myself, up there on the landing and removing my gloves. I was all liquid again. Jubilation turned to fear and I had to sit down to wait for it to pass, but it didn't, not quite.

I didn't know why I was so worried. After all, even if

I'd left perfect pictures, the Flying Squad had nothing to compare them against. My fingerprints had never been taken. I'd no criminal record.

I fidgeted and snapped. What if I'd been seen? Our neighbourhood was small – I might easily have been recognized. The kid from the Old Manor, who was having to ask his mother to cook him rice pudding because his tummy was upset.

Gradually I calmed down, the anxiety ebbed away, though when I went to collect the bags from where I'd left them, under the bushes that decorated a small roundabout in the middle of the council estate, I did hang about for what seemed like hours, outside one of those houses I'd helped rebuild, fearful that the real-life *Sweeney* counterparts of Thaw and Waterman were lurking near by ready to spring out from their souped-up Granadas. At last I called up the nerve. There was nobody. I had a hard job hefting the bags back up the hill.

In my room, I laid out the haul. There was a brass carriage clock, two silver cigarette boxes, four matched silver candlesticks, a set of silver cutlery in a box lined with red plush, a silver sweet dish, an opaque glass vase in the style of Lalique. There was a Sony cassette player and a Sony amplifier. From the jewellery boxes I pulled out two amethyst rings, a pair of pearl stud ear-rings, a single-strand pearl necklace. The pearls were real, as I discovered when I rolled them against my teeth and found their texture slightly abrasive, gritty – a trick I'd learned from a James Bond novel.

I consulted a little book my stepfather had, about gold

and silver hallmarks, and was delighted to discover, after a bit of flipping to and fro, that the silver candelabra dated from York during the middle of last century, and might be worth a lot. In one of the other jewellery boxes I found gold, three thin gold chains, and a chunky gold bracelet with twenty-three charms. There was a gold stagecoach, I remember, a gold fleur-de-lis, a gold lion, and a cat made from gold with little chips of emerald for eyes – one charm, I realized, for each of Denise Robinson's birthdays.

Suddenly I wanted to make amends, to confess, or maybe not that, but at least pack the stuff back up and leave it on the Robinsons' doorstep. Then I told myself that the Robinsons would have been insured up to the neck. By now they'd have reported the theft and it would only be inconvenient if I started monkeying with the process. They might even lose out.

Gold! I cackled like Fagin.

There was a knock on the door. 'Dick, are you all right?'

It was my mother. The silence hummed.

'You're talking to yourself,' she said.

I threw a tartan travel rug in the air and watched it settle over my treasures. 'I'm fine, Mum, thanks,' I said. 'I'll be down in a minute.'

The last time I was in England I went with my mother to look at the Old Manor, or rather, at where the Old Manor had been. Someone had knocked it down, that rambling old house. The local council's planning department had omitted to renew the protected building provision and a developer, having bought the property, used the opportunity to move in with the bulldozers.

Not all of the grounds had been levelled, though the tree stumps had been pulled up, and the lawn where we'd played croquet was now turned-over earth. The house itself had been completely razed: the study where my stepfather had worked, where I'd started tapping away myself, the low stone doorway my mother used to sail beneath, the room where I'd read through night after night of adolescent insomnia – all gone.

A new house was half up, not an ugly thing, made from the same sandstone, perhaps some of the very same old stones, as the Old Manor itself. There was a concrete mixer and a skip filled with broken glass, old window frames, and other trash. In the garage new baths, swaddled in cardboard, were ready to go into the new bathrooms.

That a house, as well as a mind, might play home to memory is what we mean by haunting. My mother and I both felt that it was a part of ourselves that had been reduced to rubble – we were in tears.

I walked up The Grove to see the house I'd burgled. The ivy was still on the wall, the stone dragons were still on guard, though the Robinsons had long since moved away. 'It was always a lovely house,' my mother said. 'But not as lovely as the Old Manor.' I wondered whether she'd say anything, whether she might remember that the Robinsons had once been robbed. She didn't; there was no reason why she should.

I got out of the car and walked between the stone dragons, up past the lawn, to the window where I'd broken in. The rose bushes had been clipped right back. It was winter. I knocked on the door, three times, but no one came, no one was at home, and so I went back down again, and there it was, gravity's pull evoking the self I'd been, the giddy thrill I'd felt, loaded with bags of stolen stuff, the little tug on the legs that made me break into a run.

Later, in Los Angeles, when Paivi asked me how I'd felt seeing the Robinsons' house again, I said I wasn't quite sure: guilty, I supposed, and embarrassed and ashamed. I also had the strange, sad feeling that this house had been allowed to remain standing, and it was because of me that my old home had been destroyed. I was even a little dottily proud for the calm head I'd been, gathering myself together after the situation had slipped on that first banana skin, the Landseer, and achieved a giddy Marx Brothers momentum.

'Proud?' she said. Her anger made me afraid, giving as it did the inkling that she was starting to see me as a different person. I was making a confession and I wasn't even sure why. It came out piece by piece. I felt impelled. My life was a torn-up map and if I lived to be a hundred I might never put all the pieces together. But certain connected fragments were coming into place; blanks which had been left in former years now assumed a granite importance.

I thought that if I told her I might start to find my way again. I'd liberate a heart that had felt, not ripped or divided, but dead until I met her.

And there was something else. At the time of our first

meeting I'd invented additional family members for myself, an extra brother and sister called David and Mary, prosaic names to give them substance and bulk. I'd elaborated on the lie, telling her that I didn't get on with them very well. There was family tension. In the aftermath of my parents' break-up they'd gone with my mother while I'd been left with my father. There they were, firm in my mind, dressed in some attributes I borrowed, others I invented for myself. David was an exaggeration of my stepbrother. He had a Ph.D. in astronomy and had built a small observatory in his suburban semi. Mary was based on a woman I'd known at Cambridge; she'd been a little older than all of us, a sexy sister.

'She bakes lemon meringues,' I'd told Paivi.

Everyone lies when they first meet a girl, I'd thought. Now I realized that I couldn't rub out this invention with the same negligent facility that I'd coloured it in. She'd say, 'Richard, you're vain and stupid and a goddammed pathological liar and I don't want anything more to do with you.' I couldn't go on the way I'd been living. I was afraid, a depression lay like lead in my stomach, and so I went on telling her other stories, other truths.

Seven

I'm going to London,' I announced, and waited for protests. None came. My stepfather shed a tear or two, while my mother looked at me with an unblinking, almost fierce expression. I had no job, no place to live, and as soon as I got off the train I took the tube to Queensway, where I'd stayed the previous summer while working for the law firm that had fired me, and checked into the first hotel I found. The room had no TV, no shower, and was so tiny there was barely room to stand up beside the bed and the wash-basin. Twelve pounds a night, in advance, but I was thrilled – the metropolitan life.

I'd experienced London as an ordeal. Before the law firm, and then my summer of bad cheques, I knew London from trips with my mother and stepfather to see West End farces and *The Black and White Minstrel Show* – or with my father: once, when I was eight, I'd lain awake in a room I was sharing with him in a hotel near Regent's Park while he argued with a prostitute over the price of a service she was about to provide. There'd been good times as well. I'd sneaked away from school to see Stanley Kubrick's *A Clockwork Orange* on the first day of its release at the big Warner cinema in Leicester Square, and for a while at university Pete had loaned me his London, which was the arcades and lobby of the Ritz, the King's Road, and cream teas in the tent at Wimbledon. Now my own London was waiting. All I had to do was invent it. I walked up teeming Queensway past the tube station and into the green of Hyde Park. It was still light, I had a book in my hand, people were out with their dogs or just strolling, and I was happy. In London I could be whatever character I chose.

I went about setting myself up as a writer.

Time Out is a weekly London magazine. Its offices at that time were in two dingy Victorian buildings facing each other. The entire ground floor of one of them was filled with back issues of the magazine, behind mountainous heaps of which huddled a gnomish figure in spectacles who stared at me reproachfully the moment I stepped through the door, as if it were his job I was after. Upstairs an enormous gas heater pumped away to no good effect in the centre of an otherwise freezing room. It was like being back at school. The overall impression was Dickensian, not radical left, which was the magazine's then reputation. A friendly American was nice to me. He reached for his keys and opened up a grey steel cupboard that stretched from floor to ceiling. This Aladdin's Cave was filled with books, and he suggested that I might choose something to review.

There was a novel called, simply, *Punk!*, in the style of the Martin Allen skinhead books, perhaps even written by the master of youth pulp himself. I do remember that *Punk!* featured descriptions of violence in which safety pins were ripped away from faces and 'blood spurted out at quite a surprising rate'.

This would have been the smart choice; i.e. the opportunity to have some fun, to demolish the thing with a few flashy strokes. But I wanted to emphasize my credentials, my seriousness, and opted instead for the plump Penguin reprint of Ronald Clark's Bertrand Russell biography.

The nice American editor raised an eyebrow. Was I qualified for the job? Hastily I babbled that I'd read philosophy at Cambridge and had already seen the book in hardcover; it was solid, a little skimpy on the early work, and it never quite struck sparks like Russell's own letters and memoirs.

'I'm not looking for a specialist review,' said the American with an air of suave disappointment. Gently, firmly, he took the book from my hands and the doors to Aladdin's Cave were swinging shut when I made a grab for two paperbacks, thrillers by Derek Marlowe.

'Read this guy?' said the American.

'No,' I said. 'Never heard of him.'

'A fresh eye is always good,' said the American. 'Get me the copy by Friday and I'll try and run it next week.'

I loved that: copy. Copy said I was in.

But copy had to be written and back at the hotel with Derek Marlowe in one hand and the current issue of *Time Out*, for September 10, 1977, in the other, I saw that copy meant problems. For a start there was the fact that in *Time Out* it seemed to be the norm to quote foreign Marxist structuralist critics, not just Althusser and Barthes (I'd heard of them), but big Russian guns such as Xudjakov, Pypin, and N. Dobroljubov. Then there was the matter of Mr Marlowe himself; the books were nimble on their feet, exciting, thoughtful and well planned, and, not imagining for a moment that these were publishable opinions for which I might get paid the same sort of cash as for a solid silver candelabra made in York by a decent artisan of the Victorian mid-century, I couldn't think of a word to say. Well, a couple of things: one of the books was set in Haiti and reminded me of Graham Greene's *The Comedians* and, more strongly, a beautiful old black and white horror film, *I Walked With a Zombie*, an RKO cheapie made by Jacques Tourneur in the 1940s. That was a start, I supposed; at least Jacques Tourneur was French.

I had no place to work and went to the British Museum to apply for a reader's ticket. But that would take a few days so I found a pub and, sitting in a corner, surrounded by mirrors which gave a sense of space and brightness, drank three or four pints while I wrote out something in longhand. Next day, having no typewriter, I went to a typing agency in a basement on Queensway, where a middle-aged blonde interrupted work on a thriller by a Belgian billionaire to transform my three scrawled pages into twenty-five neat pica lines, double-spaced on A4. She read the copy through and said it wasn't worth charging for. She'd add it to the Belgian's bill. My first review.

Needing to find somewhere cheaper to live, I looked

over the flatshare ads in the *Evening Standard*. A haughty girl in South Kensington looked at me and sniffed. A mousy girl in the same neighbourhood seemed afraid I might boil up the cat for soup. Several punks greeted me with the Johnny Rotten sneer. At a bedsit in West London, off the Shepherd's Bush Road, I was greeted by Mrs Peters, the landlady, tall and slim, smartly turned out in a tweed suit, a little worn maybe but still with a residue of style. She gave me to understand that she was a cut or two above her tenants, above me at any rate. A hardback of the new Le Carré, *The Honourable Schoolboy*, was tucked under her arm. She referred to it with nods and offhand familiarity, as if to suggest she'd been the model for one of the characters. 'Cambridge?' she said with a smile. 'I went there too, but it was a long time ago.' Her sigh hit me in the face, a minty gust of meaning. 'A *very* long time ago.'

My room was on the second floor, long and narrow, like a coffin. The steel-frame single bed sheltered beneath an impressive book shelf. 'I imagine you read,' said Mrs Peters. The carpet was green, of such a brilliant shade that an Italian designer would have hesitated to use it even in necktie-type proportion. 'It came from the Palais,' she said, meaning the ballroom down the road. There was a single gas ring, a gas fire, and a meter into which shillings had to be fed. Plaster trickled like sand from a crack in the wall. The curtains had holes in them. Wind blew from under the door, but at least there was a little fold-away desk.

Out on the landing, while I wrote a cheque for two weeks' rent in advance, a bewildered bearded face popped out from the room next door, and, without a word, popped back in again. Said Mrs Peters: 'That's Bernard. Another of my prisoners.'

The Derek Marlowe review duly appeared in *Time Out* the following week. By then my London adventure had cost more than two hundred and fifty pounds, and for this, my first published professional piece, I was to receive £7.50, not payable until the end of the month. I didn't kid myself that V. S. Pritchett was quaking in his wingtips, but I was pleased anyway. I was in print.

The British Museum was an ugly building, but had been designed by the same architect who'd done the façade at Emmanuel, a late-nineteenth-century addition, and so it felt like home. Life settled to a routine: up early, walk through the falling leaves on Holland Park Avenue, up Notting Hill Gate, straight down Oxford Street to Blooms-bury. London was golden. At the Museum a uniformed official checked my briefcase and my reader's ticket, a laminated plastic card with a photo in which, wearing a dopey grin and my stepfather's brown leather golfing jacket, I looked somewhat less than half awake.

I took a place in the circular reading room where all sound – every sliding back of a chair, each book thumping shut – flew up into the domed ceiling where some of it was absorbed before being bounced back with a gentle belch; the reading room was a stomach in which to absorb learning, a chamber filled with mysterious rumbles and echoings, terribly polite indigestion. The chairs were heavy and solid, backed with blue. The catalogues were ranged in a smaller circle at the room's hub, enormous volumes which had to be heaved out and in which titles and shelf information were pasted on little slips.

Usually I went to the North Library. Oblong lamps rose on struts out of the tables. As the day wore on I was enclosed in a golden light that seemed to have been spun from some fibre, while above there was darkness – a vast protective space. I wrote out for the umpteenth time my new novel's opening sentence.

'Crossing the Strand was an adventure – Heywood felt like a mountaineer as he walked into the pub to ask his father for a loan.'

I'd work for an hour or two, then take a walk. Passing through the dim low passage that led from the North Library to the main reading room I'd wake with a start. I'd stroll up through Bloomsbury to one of the bookshops, and, browsing through the precious, shiny new publications at the front, I'd be in dreamland again. I expected to have my novel finished and sold by Christmas.

Thursday nights were best, when the reading rooms stayed open late, after the rest of the museum had been shut down. Going out then I'd pause in the main entrance lobby. The library was behind me, illuminated manuscripts to the left, mummies and other Egyptian antiquities in the basement below. As I walked on my footsteps would echo in the marbled emptiness. I felt like an explorer.

I kept a journal, and if I didn't have my notebook with

me, wrote on whatever was to hand: envelopes, napkins, flyers handed out in the street. I wrote ideas, observations, fragments of conversation overheard in pubs or cafés.

'Really good whales.'

'Great whales.'

'*Proper* whales.'

The best time to have lived in London, these proto-yuppies continued, would have been immediately after WWII when property was so cheap they were giving it away and handing over grants to clear the bombsites. I wrote down quotes from books and from pop songs. 'Eagle flew out of the night – Peter Gabriel' went one entry, a whole page to itself. I wrote without thought and indiscriminately. I was never *not* writing. It was all the same to me. Everything seemed as good and useful as everything else. The only subject I avoided was crime, not because I thought it might be dangerous to set down a record of my robberies, or because I feared to invite bad luck. I simply didn't think to; it was as if that part of me didn't exist any more.

I had lunch with Bruce Page, formerly a leading light of the investigative team on the *Sunday Times*, soon to become editor of the *New Statesman*, almost a hero, certainly a name I knew and respected. I'd read a book he'd co-written, about the spy Kim Philby, which had led me to Graham Greene's essay on the same subject. When discovered, Philby had vanished out of his own life as if it were the *Marie Celeste*, leaving a half-empty bottle of milk in the sink of the house where he'd lived for twenty years.

Bruce Page filled my glass. He was small, friendly, and also a little fierce, glaring at me from behind spectacles with dark, heavy frames. I did my best, while telling no checkable howlers, to give an impression of not only competence, but far greater experience that I'd had.

Bruce Page might have been dazzled. He didn't say so. He blinked at me like an owl and reached for the claret. He needed help, he said; specifically he needed a researcher for a series of articles which, funnily enough, were all to do with philosophy. The fact that I'd been to Cambridge was a plus, not that Cambridge was any great shakes, but at least it wasn't – he paused for a moment – Oxford.

Bruce Page's theory was that the moral and intellectual malaise of British government, of Britain in general, was Oxford's fault, more particularly the responsibility of A. J. Ayer, whose *Language, Truth and Logic* had proposed that there were no such properties as 'good' and 'evil', merely 'boo' and 'hurrah'. Morality did not exist, only changeable codes of social acceptability. Hence: Hitler – boo!; Gandhi – hurrah!

'Oxford,' said Page, with a pert, bright look. It had been Oxford all along. Those students of the Thirties and Forties ruled the country now. A *disaster*. 'Oxford, you see.' He rattled a fork against the edge of his glass. 'Oxford.'

I was happy to learn that Oxford was to blame, though didn't have the foggiest what Bruce Page wanted me to do. Worse, I hadn't the sense to ask him right out. Such omissions were commonplace. As in other areas of my life

The Blue Suit

I was entirely failing to connect. I took the train from Euston for a job interview with the *Birmingham Post*. The editor had shirt-sleeves rolled up and a green, peaked visor protecting his print-weary eyes. He studied my CV for a moment and tossed it away. Not bothering to hide his impatience, he hauled a big fob-watch out of his pocket and asked what work I'd been doing lately.

Well, I said, I was writing a couple of reviews a week for *Time Out* and I'd just started researching a big piece of work for the *New Statesman*.

'You do realize,' he said in a brisk, brusque voice, 'that I hold both those publications in . . . *complete contempt*.'

I was being challenged: here was a chance to nail up my colours, but this was a job I wanted, needed, and the *Birmingham Post* was a solid provincial paper, good training ground. That was what my stepfather had said. The editor stared at me from beneath his green plastic visor.

'Well,' I said, straining for a compromise. 'They're a good place to begin.'

'*Tcha!*' he said.

Of course I didn't get the job. On the train going back I sat, furious, watching my reflection as we came into Euston between endless rows of terraced streets and sooty black railway sidings. Come at this way London always looked disordered, dingy. I'd spent more than forty pounds and had humiliated myself. I'd forgotten to ask for my expenses.

*

I didn't get in touch with Pete or Tony. There were further raids on the book cupboard at *Time Out*, and I did a short piece for *New Society* on London's night buses, swaying through the darkness in the soft yellow light of various upper decks, like being inside a bubble, or a galleon; but as autumn turned to winter my bank account was running low. I didn't understand London. Its parts seemed to exist each discrete from the other. Shepherd's Bush led to Holland Park to Notting Hill to Marble Arch, Oxford Street and Holborn. I knew that, because I walked it most days. But Islington? Hackney? Chiswick? How were they connected? The Tube map, with its lines crossing and intersecting, proceeding with confidence to their destinations, was a useless, indeed baffling guide to the messy sprawl of London's above ground topography. I dreamed of living in Mayfair, a paradise of pink terracotta.

At Mrs Peters's it was never quiet. Doors banged. Pipes thundered and rattled. Someone downstairs sawed away at a violin and when that wasn't going on Steely Dan or the Doobie Brothers boomed through the wall from bearded Bernard next door. Silence was something I had to stay up until two in the morning for, when the only sounds were trains in the far distance or the wail of Mrs Peters's cat, squabbling with some feline foe.

I grabbed Bernard and made him come in for tea. He was on a computer programming course for British Airways. He told me that the violinist was an Indian guy who'd lived downstairs for more than six years. He was Mrs Peters's favourite, said Bernard a little ruefully.

I was horrified: six years, here – a life sentence.

Meanwhile money continued to avoid me in the same mysterious way that girls had made their speciality. I faced the beginning freelancer's perennial problem: too little work, paid too late. A friend put me on to a cushy number, writing blurbs for videos – newfangled things back in 1977, but even in a good week I wasn't making enough to break even. My debts multiplied. In Shepherd's Bush there was a second-hand record shop that needed a sales assistant. It was a dark, poky place, smelling of rain and cigarettes. The owner was a middle-aged fellow in faded denim with long wires of grey hair that shot away on either side of his head.

'Been to college?' he asked.

'I was at Cambridge,' I said.

'Really?' he said, and made a rasping bronchial noise, a snort of derision and disbelief.

'My dad's a merchant banker,' I said, remembering another, very different interview that had taken place some months before. 'But I'd like to make a career in the music business. I'm quite happy starting at the bottom, but at the same time, and in my *spare* time of course, I'll carry on going to the clubs, looking for a band. I'm very interested in *management*. After that I'd look around for an investor. The ultimate goal would be to set up my own record label.'

I was madly articulate. None of this had crossed my mind before and yet, extemporizing this fantasy of Branson/Geffen-hood, I came not just to believe in its possibility, but actually to want this career. Slurping at his tea, the shopowner looked to the floor and shuffled his feet. In a panic I got a job at the local Wimpy, spent a day sweeping floors, couldn't bear to go back the next day and so didn't get paid for that. I thought about going on the dole, but, no, the dole was for people worse than the lofty view I had of myself.

I took some of the better looking stuff from the Robinsons' to a jeweller on High Holborn. He was an old man in a hairy tweed suit, his polka-dot bow-tie set a little skew, like a propeller about to start spinning. He inspected the gold charms on the bracelet and, one by one, the hallmarks on the four silver candlesticks. 'Is all this yours to sell?' he said, an obvious question, completely unanticipated by me, and then he offered eighty-two pounds. It was an oddly precise, and astoundingly small, sum. I said I'd been thinking more along the lines of two hundred and the old man's face took on a little angry shine. I took the eighty-two.

Afterwards, with the notes in my Mexico wallet, I felt outrage: I'd been cheated. I'd risked so much for so little. I thought about rushing back in to snatch what I could or breaking in that night.

I was earning very little and learning nothing. I rode the Underground with doctored tickets or no ticket at all. Above ground I walked fast, afraid the very buildings were trying to soak me up. My thoughts strayed aimlessly. In the street I couldn't imagine what went on behind faces. Everyone seemed hard.

The Blue Suit

I forced myself to keep busy, to keep moving, marching through the rain in an RAF greatcoat that my mother had dyed black and that began now to lose its borrowed colour. Dye trickled down my neck, dripped on to the floor of Poole's, the famous second-hand bookshop at 84 Charing Cross Road, where I went in the hope of spotting things I could sell on. One morning I got *Lolita* and two V. S. Naipauls, *Miguel Street* and *A House for Mr Biswas*, for less than three pounds. At a specialist first edition shop the proprietor offered twenty-five, more than I was expecting. I never had such good luck at Poole's again.

At lunch-time I left my briefcase behind in the British Museum and got into the habit of walking around the National Gallery, telling myself I was learning about pictures, but really in the hope that I'd meet a woman and fall in love. One day I went the other way and stopped outside the Royal Academy of Dramatic Arts to check whether anyone I knew from Cambridge was featured in the production stills outside. In Dillons, the big university bookshop, I mooched around in the second-hand department and then, as usual, at the tables near the front, where the new publications were. I walked out with the Duck-worth reprint of an Evelyn Waugh travel book, *Labels*, under my arm.

I felt them before I saw them, right between the shoulders. I was being followed, two people, a man and a woman, dressed in bulky Parkas – store detectives. If I made a run for it I could get away, down Judd Street and into the back entrance of the museum. I could lose myself there. I pictured two store detectives trying to explain themselves past security at the entrance to the reading room. It'd never happen; they didn't have tickets. I had a ticket.

Or I could walk round the corner, back into Dillons through the side entrance, dump the book, and, even if they caught up with me, deny everything. That would work too.

It was a cool, grey day, yet everything seemed crisp and too bright. A cab came towards me with its yellow light on and stopped at a zebra. I didn't move, I didn't try to move, I didn't want to move. The paving stones were huge beneath my feet.

At Tottenham Court Road police station I was put in front of a white board. A flashbulb popped. Handcuffs still on, my fingers were smeared over a black inky tablet and then pressed on to a printed sheet of paper – a box for each finger.

I wanted very much for this to be over. I'd been caught, I wasn't pretending I'd not been caught, I was offering myself up for punishment, and I wished it wouldn't take for ever. I'd been marched back into Dillons, a store detective on either side. People had looked at me with curiosity, scorn, a gladness they weren't in my shoes. The male store detective, a lanky Iranian, had made me a cup of too-sweet tea. The manager, pink in the face, asked me how many other books I'd stolen, then, eh?

The police interview room had grey lino, bilious yellow walls, and a scarred metal desk in the middle. The ceiling was low and I thought of that first time I'd visited my father in the gaol at Armley. There was the same sense of failure and drudge. I'd been told to sit so I did, on a plastic chair with spindly legs that wobbled. I waited. I waited for a long time. After a while I got up and touched the desk, quite expecting that a voice would boom from a hidden loudspeaker, 'RAYNER SIT DOWN.' My finger left an inky smudge.

I was quite certain that my fingerprints were already being cross-checked and that a Flying Squad detective was about to burst through the door and ask what I knew about a certain house near Bradford, belonged to the – ah – Robinsons. Then again I was calm, quite the card. I was mortified, scalded with shame. I was bored.

At last the door did open and a white haired giant of a man came in, a sergeant, lugging a typewriter so enormous I thought he was perhaps the only one in the station strong enough to carry it. He laid it gently on the desk, rolled in a form, and, making it clear that his own remedy for boredom was to take everything at a slow, slow pace, asked me name, date of birth, present address, phone number etc. He had a soft Irish voice. Each of my replies was met with a weary stare, a look down, an agonizingly slow picking out of letters. He didn't ask if I'd committed any other crimes. I'd have confessed to everything, anything. Instead, when he was finished, he said, 'You silly, silly man.'

The cell smelled powerfully of disinfectant. There was a mattress, but no blanket or pillow, and a toilet without seat or handle or cistern. There was a funny little dimple in the steel door where the peephole was on the other side. In the ceiling there was a single bulb, not on at the moment, protected by thick wire mesh. At the far end of the cell light filtered weakly through a grille of opaque glass. There was a constant muffled patter, footsteps. The Tottenham Court Road pavement was only a few feet above.

I sat on the bed, determined to take in every detail. They'd taken away my pens, watch, and wallet, and sealed them in a plastic bag. They'd taken away my shoe laces and my belt. This was all very interesting, I thought.

Graffiti were all over the walls, scratched by previous inmates with what instruments and ingenuity I didn't know:

GUNNERS RULE

FUCK TOTTENHAM YIDS

FUCK THE LAW

FUCK ALL COPPERS

FUCK

FUCK

FUCK

I'd be out of here in an hour or two, the sergeant had said, as soon as they'd checked my address. I'd be released on bail and would have to report to Bow Street in the

morning. I was in bright form. I sat on the edge of the bed
and examined the tiles on the wall opposite me, counting
the cracks.

I recited poetry and scenes from movies, hummed the
theme tune from the *Mr Ed* TV show, made up dialogue
in my head. It started getting dark and I was worried that
I might not get out in time to nip back to the museum and
collect my stuff.

Soon even the grey light of the grille was gone. This was
no longer interesting. 'Silly man,' the Irish sergeant had
said. 'Silly', that was right, all right; 'man' erred on the
side of flattery. I was frightened, cold in the dark, and
when I went to the door and shouted, no one came. I
thought the sergeant might have left an order that this was
to happen: give the Cambridge boy a scare.

'Turn on the light.'

I thought at least someone would hear me in one of the
adjoining cells. There was nothing; it must have been a
slow day for crime in the West End.

'TURN ON THE LIGHT, YOU FUCKERS.'

I was kept in the dark for only ten hours. I say 'only'.
No one came or went. I couldn't even have said for sure
that there *were* any other cells. For a while I thought I was
being kept in some special insulated tank. I shouted until I
was hoarse. I wept. People up on the pavement must have
heard and, though I was ashamed, knowing that I made a
sad display, I didn't stop.

*

At Bow Street the magistrate's demeanour suggested that he was shocked, frankly shocked, that I wasn't up there for trying to nab a policeman's helmet on Boat Race night. He sat high above me on his bench. He had a pink shiny face and silver half-moon spectacles over which his eyes peered at mine as he asked how I wished to plead.

'Guilty.'

'*Guilty?*' he said, as if I was trying to trick him.

'Yes, sir, guilty.'

'So you went to – ah – Cambridge, where you read philosophy and, and . . . *law*.' He gazed at me over those glittery half-moons. This was obviously another trick. 'And you work for the mmm *Time Out* and the *New* . . . yes, and the *New* . . .'

At the front sat a reporter from the local paper. Worth a story? I hoped not. In my statement I'd needlessly told all this, storing up the present humiliation.

The magistrate went on, 'You've had lots more opportunities than most of the people I see and now it seems you're in danger of turning into a thoroughly bad lot. What do you have to say for yourself?'

I said I was very sorry and it would never happen again, sir.

With a heavy sigh he examined the evidence, the book I'd tried to steal. This perked him up.

'Evelyn Waugh? When I bought this book in 1938 it cost me three shillings and sixpence.' He gave an eager look around, but no one laughed. No bother: he'd been practising law and bad jokes for forty years.

'Fined seventy-five pounds.'

By the time I left the court another defendant was up in the box, a tramp who'd got himself arrested so he could spend the night in gaol with a roof over his head, and to whose company the magistrate was wearily accustomed.

'Do you really suppose,' he asked the tramp, 'that the state can go on supporting you for ever in this manner?'

The huge court-room doors banged shut, cutting off the tramp's reply. I walked across the black and white marble lozenges of the lobby floor. There was a marble bust set in a recess of the wall, a likeness of Henry Fielding, novelist turned magistrate. It was a waterfall, drenching me with relief.

I remembered my visit to the Old Bailey the summer before last, when I'd just been a spectator and Justice Scott had turned to the jury after the trial of the young constable and said: 'Well, you can't say I didn't try.' No one had made a special plea on my behalf and I was under no illusion about having deserved one. I'd deserved just what I got: a criminal record, which disqualified me from any possibility of a career at law. It made me both angry – that it was in other people's power to judge me so – and rather happy. I promised myself that never again, ever, would I find myself where I'd just been.

I strolled into the bright chill November air, strolled along Long Acre, strolled up the Charing Cross Road, the Tottenham Court Road, strolled into Dillons and out again with another book under my arm, this time a first edition of *Dead Babies* by Martin Amis, the one with the picture of him on the back jacket, smoking a fag and looking like Mick Jagger. I strolled back, taking the route I'd expected to take the day before, into the British Museum.

That night I broke into a house down by the river in Hammersmith. I knocked on the door and, when there was no answer, went in through one of the front windows, telling myself I have it, still got it, look . . . haven't lost my nerve.

There was quiet all around, no alarm, though I knew from the Robinsons that a light was quite likely winking on a board at the local police station. I wasn't scared, despite having been in a police cell at this time the previous night. I felt excited, yet secure. I gave myself two minutes. A big dark dining-room table twinkled here and there in the yellow light from outside. There were pictures on the wall, all of them vague and incoherent in the near darkness. I had no torch. I stood by the table for a few seconds while my eyes accustomed themselves to the gloom. My ears made out sounds now – distant traffic, from Putney Bridge or the Hammersmith flyover – and when I moved, trying to tread as softly as I could, my footsteps were loud and obtrusive on the wooden floor.

From the table I lifted a candelabra, so heavy I thought it might be solid silver. On the sideboard there was a silver fruit dish from which I tipped two or three oranges and sent them bouncing across the floor. I glanced up at the pictures and didn't want to think about trying them, though they were much smaller and more manageable than the Robinsons' Landseer.

Opening a door I found myself in the hallway. A fanlight threw shadows on the marble floor. A grandfather clock was off to one side, its every tick loud as a falling spoon. I went through into another room: more pictures, furniture, and, through the window, a glimpse of the Thames, its movement captured for a moment in a bounce of reflected light. The house felt old. It had been there perhaps for centuries, always with the river flowing outside. Statesmen had passed by. Perhaps a poet had reclined in a torchlit barge on his way to Hampton Court. Cambridge had sunk not far away.

I was drifting again. I took a brass-framed photograph from a coffee table. A silver sweet dish. Reaching for a clock on top of the mantelpiece my fingers brushed against three ten-pound notes, along with a sheet of first-class stamps, lucky finds. Another small photo frame called to me from the other side of the room. Was this gold? I went quickly through another door. Glass glimmered from a cabinet in the corner. To my left there was a luminous glow, a switch. I thought, since I'd be getting out of the house anyway in a moment or two, I might as well turn on the light.

The room was filled with books. That was the impression, for even though there were shelves on only two walls and one half of another they stretched floor to ceiling. More books stood in neat piles on a table and in a small case like a spinner made from wood with a lattice frame. Two thousand books, perhaps three. A collector's room, or a writer's.

At the back of my mind when I broke into the house I

suppose there'd been the idea that this time I'd smash the place up – turn out the drawers, break the glass, gut the cushions. Simple revenge was a part of what I wanted, and now I saw its impossibility. I was shocked because I so wanted such a room myself, with a leather-topped desk, a padded swivel chair, a globe mounted on a stand in one corner, and french windows opening on to the garden. I imagined myself sitting at the desk late into the night, working by the light of a candle. I recognized some Graham Greene and Anthony Powell titles on the shelves and lifted them down. *Afternoon Men*, *The End of the Affair*. Not enough: I wished to possess the library entire, not just a portion of its contents.

It came all of a sudden but when it did this time I wasn't surprised: a siren. It might not be coming for me, I thought, but most likely it was. I picked up my bag and left the house, not bothering to close the door.

I fled London for a few days and travelled north to Scotland, to see my father. This, I suppose, was the first time I ever sought him out. I'm not sure why. I didn't have any ideas about asking his advice. I certainly wasn't going to talk to him about any of the crime. I wanted to see how he was getting on.

He was cheerful when he met me at Nairn Station, but, as we drove away, he told me his news: Connie was sick.

She lay in a bed at the end of the ward, propped up on four or five pillows. She was surrounded by flowers, magazines, and baskets of fruit, untouched, still wrapped in crinkly orange Cellophane. She was so shockingly thin and drawn it was hard to believe that this was the same woman I'd seen only twelve or so months before. She took my hand and squeezed it, as if I were her son as well, not just my father's. The rings were loose on her wasted fingers. She was wearing the diamond band I'd thought about stealing that night from the bathroom, when the street lamps had shone through the frosted glass like spangles.

We talked about Cambridge. She told me what a lovely time they'd had there, and how much it had meant to my father. He, meanwhile, smoothed the sheets on the bed, went away to get some water for the flowers, chatted with the ward sister, and replenished a jug of orange juice.

It was stomach cancer, he explained when we were in the car again, the same as Nanna Wrose.

That night I helped him and the hotel chef get dinner ready. I shelled peas and fed carrots into the blender while he encouraged me to flirt with one of the waitresses. In the kitchens there was a faint and unpleasant smell of grease, as if the pans and ovens had been used for so many years they could never be scrubbed quite clean. With a frying pan in his hand my father paused for a moment, and glanced up to the ceiling, sad.

Graham, marginally the less dour of Connie's two sons, the Brothers Grimm, turned up later. We sat on high stools at the bar. We gulped whisky and Coke, and when my father reached over to help himself to another double,

Graham said, his voice an admiring murmur: 'Your dad's been a rock.'

My father smiled, raising his glass. He was full of plans for the future. When Connie was well again they were going to build an extension to the hotel, fifteen new rooms with bathrooms *en suite*; this would ensure an extra star from the AA and the RAC, and thus attract more guests. But the two of them would take a holiday first. He thought Copenhagen. 'I'll show Connie the Mermaid, she'll love it,' he said, and Graham and I raised a glass to that.

The next day we went for a drive, a 'spin' as my father always called it, the first we'd taken together in more than ten years. The last time would have been North Wales, bowling over the Conwy Suspension Bridge in an Aston Martin. I realized I'd spent far more time with him in cars than anywhere else. There'd been those dodgy and quite probably dangerous trips through Pennine snow to visit my grandparents; the journeys cross-country to meet in hotels where I'd be handed over to my mother and stepfather, occasions he negotiated drunk, and always late; junkets to Manchester, where the *Daily Express* building was lit up like an ocean liner in the night. 'Look,' he'd say, pointing to the running presses, 'tomorrow's fish and chips.' Every house he ever lived in looked as though he'd moved in the previous day and could move out again within the hour. Home, for my father, was a motor car, or a pub.

On that morning we drove only as far as the eastern Scottish coast. We stopped on the promenade to chat and look out over the sea. I don't remember what we spoke of.

What I remember is that I felt very much his son. I loved him. A trawler was heading south, rolling and pitching, butting the sea.

In London there were fogs and red skies above the Hammersmith Broadway, as if the sky were on fire south of the river. At *Time Out* the square steel heater bubbled and boiled away and a nasal voice droned: 'The trouble with all the bloody television critics in this country is that they write about TV as if it were just a great big book.' I didn't quite see what was wrong with that, so long as you didn't assume TV *was* a great big book, but said nothing. I was happy to be up here, holding an advance copy of next week's issue with Dennis Potter on the cover.

'Reliability and competence,' said my American friend. 'That's what I'm looking for. Anything else is a bonus.'

I wanted to protest: what about style, insight, gags? What about readability, something that *Time Out* seemed a little short on, what about that then, eh? Again I was afraid to pipe up, busy as I was in front of the cupboard, looking over the new stuff, amazed as usual by just how much did come out. Biographies, histories, memoirs, obscure and not-so Ph.D. theses, memoirs, guides, how-tos, ABCs of, an absolute deluge of new novels every week. I wasn't discouraged. To publish a book was the greatest happiness I wished for from life. As to reviewing them, I'd soon picked up on the old hack's wisdom. When asked what sort of books I liked I said: 'Short ones.' At *Time*

Out we were campaigning for the fifty-thousand-word maximum.

I met Guillermo Cabrera Infante through a friend, who asked if I'd heard that the author of *Tres Tristes Tigres*, one of the great Latin American novels of the 1960s, was living in London now, in superb exile on the Gloucester Road. It seemed unlikely – the Gloucester Road? – but I made an appointment and was greeted at the door by a small spruce man with the dapper impishness of Chaplin. His goatee beard and little round wire-rimmed glasses conveyed high seriousness and slapstick both.

In the living-room there was a huge portrait of a younger Guillermo, sitting in an armchair with a beautiful dark-haired woman at his shoulder. Bookshelves of triangular black steel stretched along the entire length of one wall. Moments later a woman appeared, the beauty from the picture, his wife, and I sat with a cup of espresso balanced on my knee while Guillermo's eyes peered and pierced from behind those little glasses. He was delighted to learn that I'd been born in Bingley, near Haworth, and that many hours of my childhood had been spent on the Brontë moor. He took me into another room, his den, where there was a poster on the wall, for Luis Buñuel's version of *Wuthering Heights*. He told me about a scene in the movie where an old man read to a child. He reached down a Bible from another of those weird steel shelves and read the passage in question.

' "For we are born of nothing, and after this we shall be as if we had not been; for the breath in our nostrils is smoke: and speech a spark to move our heart.

"Which being put out, our body shall be ashes, and our spirit shall be poured abroad as soft air, and our life shall pass away as the trace of a cloud, and shall be dispersed as a mist, which is driven away by the beams of the sun and overpowered with the heat thereof.

"And our name in time shall be forgotten, and no man shall have any remembrance of our works."'

Guillermo paused, sighed, went on. He spoke with a heavy accent.

'"Come therefore, and let us enjoy the good things that are present, and let us speedily use the creatures as in youth.

"Let us fill ourselves with costly wine and ointments: and let not the flower of the time pass by us.

"Let us crown ourselves with roses, before they be withered: let no meadow escape our riot.

"Let none of us go without his part in luxury: let us everywhere leave tokens of joy: for this is our portion, and this is our lot."'

With a smile Guillermo put down the book, and I wasn't sure what to say. Was he teasing me or was this a test of some kind? I said I thought the passage very beautiful.

The Wisdom of Solomon, he said, book 2, verses 2–9, a statement of atheism so forceful the authors of the King James version had placed it in the mouth of a madman, a thief. He picked up the book and read again, from a later passage where Solomon himself was speaking: '"For the hope of the ungodly is like dust that is blown away with the wind; like a thin froth that is driven away with the storm; like as the smoke that is dispersed here and there with a tempest, and passeth away as the remembrance of a guest that tarrieth but a day."'

Guillermo smiled mischievously over his gold spectacles. For an awful moment I wondered if my friend somehow knew what I'd been up to and had told him. That was silly. Here was simply a man who'd been able to spot my dreams and dilemmas, those of the young man in a hurry.

He told me that if I wanted to learn about cinema London was at that moment the best city in Europe to do it. 'Wonderful repertory theatres. The Scala. The Electric. You must go,' he said, wagging his finger. 'Each afternoon. You must be a student of cinema and books and, most important, the real world. You must be prepared to fight a battle, and not retreat at the first, or even the hundredth, difficulty.'

He said all this lightly, as if announcing it were of no more importance than the colour of his shirt; but then Guillermo, in his natty black suit, was obviously meticulous in matters sartorial. He gave me an American copy of his novel, as then unpublished in England. 'Please don't try to learn anything from this,' he said. 'I broke all the rules. It's better that you learn them first before you do that.'

Afterwards, when I'd walked a hundred yards or so towards the tube station, I paused to look at the book. The Spanish title was *Tres Tristes Tigres*, its English rendering *Three Trapped Tigers*, those sad cats locked up to preserve the tongue-twister. Some five hundred pages long, the winner of big literary prizes in France, Italy, Spain, it had taken him a decade to write. You didn't thieve your way into the party.

I hadn't yearned for the London life. I hadn't pored over maps, learning short cuts up narrow lanes and back-streets. I'd gone there without much of a plan but with the assumption that everything would fall into place. I would find myself. It wasn't happening. I had friends who lived in squats, near-derelict terraced houses with overgrown gardens, the floorboards ripped up, and posters of Marx and Engels on the walls. I had arguments with them about the likelihood of revolution, and whether what the Provisional IRA was up to on the streets of Londonderry might justly be described as historically inevitable. They thought I was a liberal, all right, but a bit of a toff. On the other hand I also knew the Cambridge and Chelsea crowds, with their flats in the posher parts of town. I argued with them about books and wine and the merits of the sweeper system versus 4-2-4 in football. They thought I was a leftie, all right, but a bit of an oik. I was still the boy who believed in nothing and could argue any position. I hoisted up whatever sail as the occasion arose.

I kept my booty from the robberies in various places. Half the stuff from the Robinsons was still in one of the canvas bags, hidden at my mother and stepfather's; I'd even left one or two items – a silver cigarette box, the Lalique vase – on quite open display. The rest was with me in London, with the additions of the candelabra, the sweet dish, and the other bits and bobs from the Hammer-smith house. Most of this was locked in a suitcase on the top shelf of my wardrobe, where Mrs Peters never dusted, but the jewellery was tucked in various envelopes for which I had hiding places all around my room: in the desk, the pockets of my jackets, in an empty coffee jar.

I gave a pair of black *diamanté* ear-rings to Mrs Peters, who was pleased, and very puzzled, and a pair of lovely green jade ones to Tahlia, who I met at a party in north London. Most of the other women had on black plastic bin-liners held up with safety pins while she, daringly, wore a white man's shirt and faded Levi's. She had lustrous red hair and pale skin, an ethereal Pre-Raphaelite look. Her father was an actor who resembled another, more famous, for whom I mistook him. She was sixteen, the kind of girl Cambridge had primed me to impress. The next night I picked her up from her grandparents – they lived in Knightsbridge, a big-doored house with a blue plaque and a broad sweeping stairway. The walls were like an art gallery, a little Jeu de Paume: there was a Degas, a Millais, a dinky Renoir with lots of violet flowers. Over dinner Tahlia told me about Grandpa and the pictures. 'He gets in a frightful tizz if I want to bring someone new to the house. He has to have them checked out.'

'Excuse me?'

'By the police. Now don't look stuffy. It's the same for everyone.'

Almost choking on fettucini alfredo, I had that image again, of a machine somewhere clicking away through millions of sets of fingerprints, making inexorable progress towards those beneath my name.

'You sailed through,' Tahlia said. 'Don't worry.' I was desperate to fall in love, and she was the loveliest, sweetest girl I'd met since Janie, rich obviously, but too young, too easy – I thought I needed more of a challenge. I was interested in the Renoir, however. The problem with breaking into houses at random was that I never knew what I was going to get. The risk was disproportionate to the prospect of gain. But a Renoir? I liked the idea.

All fired up again by meeting Guillermo, I set back to work on my novel.

'Heywood was a tall young man, his hair something between rust and curry powder. The best that really could be said for him is that he looked as if his father might possibly have been a gentleman. Appearances can be deceptive. He inserted a nail-file in the gap between the windows and pushed upwards to catch the lock. The windows opened and he entered the study.'

Heywood had been given a gun and hired to kill a man, into whose house he was now breaking, and who was to turn out to be none other than his own father – they also hadn't seen each other in years. Yet I was quite blind to the obviousness with which the superstructure of all this pushed up from crime and my relationship with my father, from my sunken life. I neither saw nor even sensed it. The story, in the writing, seemed disconnected from any reality I knew about; it was a fantasy whisked up from other books, Chandler with dollops of Camus spooned in.

I had lunch again with Bruce Page. He wore a bright

tweed jacket like a bookie's and he waved his hands a lot as he expounded further details of his theory. Moral philosophy was from the days of Socrates regarded as an attempt to think out the issues involved in conduct, for the sake of acting better. But logical positivism – first associated with Cambridge and Ludwig Wittgenstein but later, through A. J. Ayer, taking fashionable, *devastating* hold at Oxford – had announced this a mistake, saying, if it interests you to study this, then do, but don't think it will be any use. It's just a game. Thus Oxford had trained up generations of dupes, fine minds, liable to be taken in by any moral adventurer. Philosophy had been hijacked, and the English ruling class followed like the container behind a lorry. He'd grasped a strand of something bigger, what Jung called the century's loss of religious sense, and he wanted me to follow it like an investigative story, like a lead. 'Facts,' he said. 'Talk to people,' he said. 'Civil servants. MPs.'

I felt the way I had meeting Guillermo. I was being given help, tokens, clues, and I didn't know how to use them. I still couldn't get into the garden.

Page signalled a little mournfully for another bottle. 'My staff, they seem to think it's a joke,' he said. 'But then they all *went* to Oxford.'

I got hold of the names of three or four researchers in the House of Commons, made appointments to go and see them, and, later, perhaps, depending on how that went, their MPs as well. I put on the blue suit and went to Westminster. For a few days I had interviews in panelled committee rooms where at first I felt the way I had in the banks, expecting a hand on my shoulder. I'd be thrown out and declared a fraud. After a little while I realized that the *New Statesman*, the grand and most certainly arcane nature of the investigation, my suit, all these combined to provide an authority; I became the eager reporter, asking: Was Britain in bad shape? Had there been, somewhere along the line, a more or less collective failure of principle and morality among the ruling élite?

The very fact that I was asking these questions was another irony that went sailing by. I sat in the canteen, reading, or chatting with a researcher who worked for a Labour MP from the Midlands. She told me that because politics made the country work, the art of politics was the only work worthwhile; politics was where the action was, and I began to think about a career in this area. Why not? I had strong memories of a TV series based on the political novels of Anthony Trollope. One character, a raffish young man, had made a brilliant and rapid start, ruined himself, committed suicide. Another, more dogged, had won through in the end. Or had it been the other way round? Either way I was failing to see a point that had been made about the fragility of endeavour. Small choices, perhaps not even choices – a remark, the wearing of a certain jacket, an unintended snub – have a habit of leading very logically to large and unwished-for consequences. Dreams are dispersed by the wind of reality.

My understanding of politics was that you had to speak
well, think nimbly on your feet, and announce with great
earnestness principles which would later vanish like
vapour from the mind. I thought I could perform pretty
well in those areas.

The different segments of my life continued to whirl
about. I walked, from Shepherd's Bush to Westminster in
the morning, to the British Museum, to one of the parks
at lunch time, then back to my room again at night, and if
this wasn't enough I ran, unable to keep still. Movement
wasn't only a ruse to keep boredom at bay. Some part of
me sensed that I'd sink if I stopped even for a moment.
When in doubt I fell back on books. One Saturday, restless
in my room at about 4.30 in the afternoon, I went to the
phone, called a friend and asked, then begged him to drive
me to Cambridge so I could go on a spree. We raced up
on the motorway and arrived with so little time to spare
before Heffer's closed that I almost had to grab at random
from the shelves. In London I hunted all over, stealing
Anthony Powell's *At Lady Molly's* and *Casanova's
Chinese Restaurant* in first edition, as well as the Heinemann reprint of Powell's study of the biographer John
Aubrey, whose *Brief Lives* was an electric record of
Englishmen and English ways in the seventeenth century
at the time of the Civil War. I searched for a rare 1930s
copy of the *Lives* edited by John Collier who, I learned
both from Anthony Burgess's *Urgent Copy* and from John
Updike's *Picked Up Pieces* (the Knopf edition – what was
that doing in Deptford?) had written an eccentric screen-
play of *Paradise Lost*, as well as various short-story

collections to search for and steal. In Foyle's one afternoon I caught sight of a lanky fellow wearing a bulky Parka, his familiar face glancing over a pile of books with no great absorption – the store detective by whom I'd been caught. He turned away, embarrassed, not because he'd recognized me, but because he'd let a customer spot what he was at. I walked out with the paperback I had in my hand, the new Penguin Modern Classics edition of *The Portrait of a Lady*, not so pretty as the old one with the grey spine.

All this bustle had one effect: I started falling asleep in the British Museum. I'd go in, order some books from the catalogue, settle myself on one of the blue-backed chairs, and start to work. I'd make some notes on the *New Statesman* thing, or plug away at my novel, where Heywood had failed to murder his father and was now stranded at Waterloo Station. He didn't want to move. He lay on his bench and stared at the station clock, perhaps hoping to send down roots and start reaching up towards it. I had no idea myself about where he should go and after a minute or so of trying to push him on I'd feel my head grow heavy. Next thing I'd be waking up not sure who or where I was, startled, and surrounded by the digestive rumblings of the British Museum's mighty belly – chairs sliding, books closing with soft detonations. The books I'd requested myself would be at my elbow, order slips poking out like little white slats. It was the one place in London where I knew absolute peace and soon I couldn't not sleep there; it was like a drug, or an illness, like my migraine. This went on for weeks.

I started taking my notebook to a snack bar nearby.

The windows were steamed up, the red plastic benches narrow and cramped. In my greatcoat I was like a bear trying to squeeze myself down at a picnic table. So mostly I walked, through a London that was cold, grey, and wet. Sodden scraps of paper adhered to the pavements and to the soles of my shoes. A high-rise office block stood empty on the Tottenham Court Road. The caretaker left a few lights on when it grew dark, always in a different part of the building, now on the tenth floor, now up on the thirty-fifth, as if he were sending out a message. If I thought of my father at all it was with sadness. I hoped he and Connie did get to go to Copenhagen. He'd driven there once during one of his big-time motor rallies. This had been in the late 1950s. The famous driver Paddy Hopkirk had taken part in the same event. There's a picture of him with my father leaning up against a car, an orange Saab, round and bright as a dream. 'Don't get into debt, son,' he'd said, before I'd left Scotland. 'He'll kill you, will Dr Debt.'

I was coming to know London a little better. I found an old church I liked to go to. From the outside it seemed narrow and grubby white, with an inappropriately tall spire squeezed out between rows of terraced houses. It had been damaged by a bomb during WWII and was no longer used for religion. The basement was a homeless shelter.

The rails of the pulpit were plain oak. From here the church's exterior ungainliness was transformed to proportion and grace. There were no benches, no seats or prayer stools, no furnishings of any kind, but shafts of light flooded in from the tall windows on either side and met at the precise centre of the church. Smells of dust and smashed stone mingled in the atmosphere. There were memorials and tombs on the worn flags within the cloisters. It reminded me of Cambridge.

One afternoon before Christmas I stood in there and reviewed how I was doing. I'd made some progress on the writing front, but it hadn't been spectacular. I wasn't exactly flying. My debt had doubled and more, I was living in a crummy bedsit, and the Bursar at Emmanuel College had written again, raising the old issue of £652.75 – the unpaid bill. Unless it was paid within twenty-eight days, he said, my degree would be taken away. Could they really do it? Theft seemed to be the only thing I was any good at. I was pleased that although I'd been caught, gaoled, prosecuted, my nerve was holding up. I didn't know I'd glanced the iceberg and was skimming, cruising, waiting for the merest bump to take me down.

Eight

I was born in 1955, at four in the morning on December 15th. Ten days premature, I was long, thin, and of wrinkled red appearance. I weighed less than four pounds.

'Tha'll never raise *that*,' the midwife said.

'Watch me,' my mother replied.

My earliest memories are all of her. On laundry day I was cosy in the kitchen with the smell of hot linen, the clatter of the iron on the stand, and the faint *thud-thud-thud* on the ironing board. On Friday afternoons we took the trolley-bus to Bradford and did the week's shopping at the stalls in the covered markets. You could buy almost anything there – not only fruit, meat, and vegetables. There was a stall with a thousand different sizes of nuts and bolts, and another with opened boxes of Turkish delight, hints of pink flesh behind the sweet white frosting. There were handbags, umbrellas, coal scuttles, lawn-mowers and garden gnomes with bobble-hats and red noses. They were great mysterious bazaars. Gas lamps hissed and blood dripped from the ceiling where chickens and pheasants hung in the darkness of the rafters. At Brown-Muffs, the big department store, cash disappeared into tubes, sucked away with a pneumatic *whoosh*. More magic! Upstairs, in the tea-rooms, women were bundled up in their thick winter coats like teddy bears with failed soufflés for hats. I remember once, in the middle of the afternoon, we went into a church. It was huge and black, with the Bradford sky sailing above. There was another crisis, something to do with my father, and my mother gripped my hand as she said: 'You pray too. Pray for us, Dick, pray as hard as you can.'

She hit me, not slaps; she belted me into the middle of next week, to use her own phrase. When I was really bad she'd lock me in my room or the coal cellar. Security and sudden alarm – these are the associations.

She came from a Bradford working-class family. Her father, Harry, was an engineer in the mills, where he maintained and repaired the big weaving machines; but at home it was Nellie, her mother, who ruled. Nellie's eye missed nothing; her tongue was a weapon. 'Harry,' she'd say, 'don't tell me yer've bin reading that newspaper again. Yer'll fill yer 'ead so full o' ideas it'll mebbe burst. Wouldn't tek much.' I saw Nellie smile, once, on the occasion of the Queen Mother's visit to Bradford in 1962.

They lived in a semi-detached with a huge circular cricket field at the back. This house became so known to me, so familiar and loved, that if I went back now I'm sure I'd find some evidence of my childhood, a toy car or a cricket bat sticky with the linseed oil I used to rub in; and if I could put the two mirrors back in their places on the walls of the living-room, facing one another, I'd swim back through time and make everything right.

My mother is fiery and determined, with ginger hair and a temper to match. She has a brisk, businesslike walk, more of a boxer's march across the ring. When she was twelve she won a scholarship to Bradford Grammar School, no small feat then or now; she didn't go because Nellie wouldn't spend the twelve pounds a year necessary for a uniform. It was a needless extravagance, Nellie told her, yet when Nellie was on holiday she never strolled the promenade of Blackpool or Bridlington with less than two hundred pounds in her handbag, a fortune in those days, in case she saw something she fancied. The point about the uniform, as my mother came to realize – a bitterness she carried with her, a sense that she was denied her chance – was that twelve pounds was a needless extravagance *for a girl*.

When she married my father, on August 17th, 1945, it seemed like a big step up. He was handsome, a dashing RAF officer with a business of his own. Soon after my sister was born, a little more than a year later, my mother picked up the phone and heard a stranger's voice, female, asking if she knew about the other woman my father was 'keeping in Riddlesden', a town only two or three miles away. He'd rented a flat and was giving the woman twenty-five pounds a week. No wonder money was always tight. My mother looked out from our dining-room over the walled garden, where there was a tennis court and an oak tree, two hundred years old. She was flattened, my father made suddenly alien to her. She'd been ripped from her skin and he'd become someone else.

She'd grown up in the Depression and it was made clear to her by her parents that the best she could hope for was marriage. Thus my father had seemed a decent bet, which didn't make good, though she spent twenty years trying. She once told me she thought she'd have killed herself if she'd stayed with him another minute. Yet her decisions, once made, seem almost offhand. Likewise many of her attitudes: the good past, for instance, was useful, because a comfort; the bad past wasn't and therefore didn't exist. Both she and my stepfather referred to their marriage as a compromise, a coming together of dented suitcases. I believed, needed to believe, that it was more, that they loved each other, had healed each other, redeemed each other in some way.

My parents were divorced in 1951 and I was born, as I've said, in 1955. No one informed me of the anomaly until the time that I'm writing about, when I was in my early twenties, and my brother Keith said that, by the way, did I know I was a bastard? It was left to my father to reveal the precise circumstances of my conception. At around midnight, on March 20th, 1955, there was a reconciliation in the back of a Rover motor car, he reported. My mother had never been more passionate.

The real surprise, I suppose, would have been to learn that he'd invested in a pension plan, say, or that she'd joined the Conservative Party. Besides, all this rather suited the idea I was forming of myself – the changeling, the bastard son. It gave me licence, and I wanted very much the excuse to behave as I pleased.

Aged ten I'd drive her batty singing the same lines of a Rolling Stones song over and over, 'Here it comes, here it comes, here *comes* your nineteenth nervous breakdown.' As a teenager I was really able to get her going calling her 'Mrs Morel', after the hero's suffocating mother in *Sons and Lovers*.

These days, in California, I'm on the phone six thousand miles away, and it doesn't take hours any more. D. H. Lawrence isn't required. I've honed the technique, and now I need only the words, 'I've never been a part of the family.'

That Christmas, after my first five months in London, I travelled north. The train was stopped – snow on the line, and after that there was a coach, which broke down in Skipton, fifteen miles from home. Snow fell heavily, more was on the way, and when I called to see if someone might come and pick me up my stepfather said, no, the weather was too bad.

I could have ordered a taxi and asked my stepfather to pay at the other end. He would have, but I knew he'd have made a scene about it, and no one was going to steal my limelight on that night. I'll walk, I thought, and if I freeze to death, then they'll be sorry. Thus armoured, I bundled myself into my RAF greatcoat and set off into the snow.

The Blue Suit

For a start it was over an hour before the twinkling lights of the last council estate fell behind me and I came upon the sign announcing Skipton's outer limits. After that there was an hour or more of open country before I reached Bolton Abbey, in whose ruins Janie and I had, during our second Cambridge year, once made love. By this time the front of me was entirely covered in snow. Snow melted on my lips and eyelids but stuck to the rest of me. Snow drove itself up my nostrils and into my trouser legs. Snow numbed my cheeks and flayed the tips of my ears. I'd hoped that constant movement would keep me warm. I was wrong.

From time to time a car crept up, windscreen wipers furious, the blizzard sliced and briefly swirling in its headlights. When that happened I made a half-hearted effort to put out my thumb, but I didn't really want anyone to stop, and no one did. I trudged on, or rather I crunched on, leaving tracks behind me. Eventually I had to move my march to the centre of the road itself, because snow was starting to drift on the pavements. By then it was the middle of the night and there was no more traffic anyway. I kept having to stop, take off my greatcoat, shake loose the latest dusting, and put on another layer of clothing – a second shirt, a third one, a jacket, a sweater – then the dampening greatcoat back on top of all that, until at last I was swaddled like the Michelin man.

The great trek from Skipton took some five or six hours. Only after three in the morning did I walk up the driveway of the Old Manor and see that the light in the living-room was still on. So was the light in the dining-room, the light in the kitchen, the light in the study. All the upstairs lights were on as well. The house was ablaze like a beacon, and the front door was open. A little heap of snow was melting on the blue hallway carpet.

My stepfather was waiting in the living-room. We'd always got on well. He was a tall man, a streak of bacon with jet-black hair. When I'd been a child he'd seemed a bit forbidding, a distant giant, though he could be great fun as well, especially on holidays abroad when he appeared on the beaches of the Adriatic and Mediterranean still dressed in a three-piece suit and approached Italian bandmasters to demand the playing of his favourite song, 'Velia' by Franz Lehar, to which he would sing along, blissfully tuneless. Demands from foreigners he met with an imperious English '*What!*', or '*What! What!*', or on especially dire occasions, '*What! What! What!*' An accomplished man, he'd been an officer in the merchant navy, a newspaper editor, a columnist. He was no match at all for my mother in the tantrum department.

'She's drunk,' he said. 'She hasn't stopped drinking since you called. She's been chasing me around the garden with a carving knife.'

She'd assured him that she'd been sleeping with this same knife under her pillow for the last ten years, in case he tried anything. It seemed unlikely, but then with my mother you never knew. I was assumed to be the only member of the family who could control her when she was like this. Some years before, during a similar episode, I'd found myself saying, 'Mother, stop being so bloody stupid.' Much to my surprise, and her own, she had stopped. She'd meekly accepted a cup of tea.

Footsteps thundered across the oaken floor of the bedroom upstairs.

'How's the writing going?' said my stepfather, with an attempt at brightness. In the 1950s he'd published a novel, the comic tale of a young Yorkshireman's sentimental education. A movie had been based on the book, starring blonde bombshell Diana Dors; she'd been part of the education. In one scene a portrait of the hero's dead father had spoken to him from the wall, admonishing him not to squander his money, his chances. 'Think of your market,' said my stepfather. 'Comedy's best.'

Meanwhile upstairs my mother stopped suddenly with her thumping. There was silence. The varnished Canaletto reproduction gleamed above the stone fireplace. Coals shifted in the open grate. 'What the bloody hell is she doing now?' said my stepfather, plucking nervously at his suit lapel.

Outside a car whispered through the snow. From the door I saw that it was going up The Grove, towards the Robinsons' house. I was in a daze, curious about what would happen, when my mother at last put in her appearance, sweeping down the stairs with the knife in one hand and a half-empty bottle of Gordon's in the other. 'Fasten your safety belts,' she said. 'It's going to be a bumpy night.'

I was too exhausted to plan. I wasn't thinking. I felt I

had to match my mother's mood with something mad of my own. I went to the kitchen and drew another knife from the kitchen drawer, a vicious looking thing with a six-inch blade. I came back and stuck it against my mother's throat.

'You've no idea how desperate I am,' I said.

This was one moment that never did get transformed into family lore, though my mother and I did eventually speak about it, years later, when she was the one who remembered that self-dramatizing corker of a final line. I still don't know how to weigh what happened that night; I'm ashamed, yet not sorry, if that makes sense, and if asked to name two memories that crystallized my relationship with my mother, then sitting cosy in the kitchen while she worked a hissing iron would be first, and this the second. It's been hard for me to get to know her, to forgive her, I suppose, for being my mother. We've always fought, we've always been close. For years I thought I was the product of my father solely; another error.

'You worry me, dear,' she said the next morning, and she wasn't even talking about my holding the knife to her throat. She was talking about London, and what I was and wasn't doing there. 'I've been wondering about the things in the spare room.'

We were in the kitchen. I had my nose as usual in the pages of the *Daily Telegraph*.

She said, 'There's a lot of stuff up there. In boxes. All wrapped up in newspaper.'

It was only now that this really sank in: she'd found the rest of the stuff from the Robinsons'. I wanted to protest that she *never* went into the spare room. I felt panic rise and flutter in my chest. I was thirteen again, and she was coming along the corridor towards my bedroom to surprise me with my cache of Raquel Welch pictures.

'Oh, that,' I said, buying time. I sipped at my tea, made the way only my mother seems to like or indeed know how, stewed treacle dark and thick as varnish. 'You mean that stuff.'

I felt as I often did when talking to her: Caliban captive within a sense of worked-for ease. I was the only person I knew who'd been to see *Easy Rider*, that archetype of groovy adolescent rebellion, *with his own mother*. How had this happened? I can't remember. 'Oh yes,' she'd said. 'It was jolly good, wasn't it? I liked that. Motorcycles, yes, and what was that stuff they were smoking?'

As my mind raced to come up with a story my stepfather peeped around the door, a little sheepishly, amazed that the two knife merchants were talking to each other. He needn't have worried. Last night had been a little too much of a carry-on: me as would-be Hamlet, my mother as Gertrude played by Bette Davis – these were taxing roles. 'Breakfast?' he said.

I was off the hook and when, towards the end of the holiday, my mother brought up the subject again, I had a story roughed out. 'I got interested in collecting nice things,' I said. 'Expensive things. Like the books.' This, I told her, was how I'd spent all the money from my university grant.

She blinked. 'But what about your tuition fees? Your college bills?'

'I haven't paid them,' I said. 'They're going to take away my degree.'

The confession left her speechless, and she never referred to the loot in the spare room again.

Nine

I'd been back in London a month and had ignored Emmanuel's deadline. Instead I'd followed Guillermo's advice and come down with film fever, which entailed entire days at the Scala repertory theatre, swimming in double or sometimes triple bills of Howard Hawks, Douglas Sirk, Nicholas Ray. In some former life the Scala had been a zoology museum. The walls were decorated with paintings of lions and baboons, and the auditorium stank of urine, sprayed about by the cat whose job it was to keep the rodents at bay. At least it was warm in there.

London was frozen over. The Christmas snow had started to thaw when another cold snap had covered the pavements with a treacherous grey lacework of ice. My room at Mrs Peters's was more dismal than ever, and letters arrived from my mother on a regular basis, begging me to find a job, any job. Having done all that research for Bruce Page's project about the moral decay of British thought and government, I'd failed to deliver my notes.

I was oddly unworried.

One night Pete and I went out to dinner. He was dressed in a pinstriped suit and one of those shirts with the bright stripes from Jermyn Street. The shirt was open at the collar and he wore no tie. 'The Crisp Baron,' he said, pulling a face. I had it at the back of my mind to ask him for some money. 'Did you hear about Gordon?' he said. 'He committed suicide.'

I gulped at my wine. The last time I'd seen Gordon had been at Cambridge; he'd been lying on the floor of someone else's room, talking about *Romeo and Juliet*. He'd been the best student actor of our time there, destined for stardom, we all knew.

'He jumped in front of a train,' said Pete. 'No one knows why.' We looked at each other, trying to measure our reactions. There was a moment of sadness and then a shared guilty something else, glee almost. A gifted peer had taken his own life – it seemed impossible, and yet we'd guessed it would happen to at least one of our gang. I felt sorrow and at the same time relief. The candle shimmered on the table.

Dinner ended with repeated bursts of laughter. We talked about the new play by Harold Pinter. We talked about the latest novels and whether we'd be going to Glyndebourne in the summer. We talked about ourselves, and how well we were doing. Pete thought I was other than I was, and I wanted very much to be what he thought. I didn't ask for the money.

Drunk, the two of us tumbled into a cab and went to a

party, on Pete's patch, down in Chelsea, and it was there that I met Chrissie, a skinny and stylish blonde, dressed, not to kill, but with impeccable panache, in a black and white checkerboard dress and a leather jacket. She had long legs, neat smallish features, and slender buttocks with the slight swell and cleft of a peach. Pete knew her, of course. She'd lived in New York for a couple of years; she'd been wild, code for a suspicion or fantasy that she'd behaved the way we'd like to ourselves. 'She dropped out of sight for a while. Now? I don't know. You'll never fuck her,' he said, which I took only to mean that he hadn't. I thought I could learn something from this woman.

I spoke to her, and got her to write her phone number in one of the notebooks I always carried, but when I called the next day it was someone else who answered. 'Oh no,' said this other female voice. 'Chris doesn't *live* here. I think she went to Natasha's today.'

Natasha had different information. 'Chrissie? Isn't she at her brother's?'

The brother answered with a careless flick. 'Yeah, she's here.' He didn't bother to cover the phone. 'CHRIS! Some bloke.'

We met for dinner. The restaurant was expensive, Italian, of her choice. She kept me cooling my heels for twenty minutes or so, a habit of hers, and when she made her entrance it was with slow, indolent strides, letting the room watch. She wore a short dress of crushed red velvet, flat black shoes, and over her shoulder she toted an ugly satchel of worn black leather, as if she weren't quite sure

whether the evening would end up with a long-distance
hike.

I couldn't help glancing around. Chrissie wore her
sexuality deadpan like a comic: I know my effect on you,
on men, she seemed to say, and frankly I'm amused more
than anything else – now let's look past that.

'I heard you were in New York.'

'Who told you that?'

'A friend.'

She picked up a green match-book that was positioned
like a little tent on the table and gave it to me to light her
cigarette. 'So what else did you find out about me from
Peter Josephson?'

'He said you were wild.'

'Not any more,' she said matter-of-factly. Her hands
were less than elegant, I noticed – the nails bitten down,
the fingers swollen and even a little blue. 'What's their
place in Norfolk like?'

And so it went on. Everything I said something came
back with a little extra fizz and spin. She wanted to hear
stories, about people, not anecdotes. She was interested in
the forts people built around themselves and the money
they used to do it. If people didn't have any kind of a fort
– if somehow they'd fallen from the battlements or had
never aspired to climb them – she was interested in that
too.

If Pete had been a girl I suppose I'd have wanted to have
an affair with him and now, in Chrissie, I'd found his
female counterpart: glamorous, arrogant, wise in the ways

of a world to which I wished very much to belong. 'You have no fort and perhaps you never will,' she said. 'Pete has a fort. New money. You're much more interesting than he'll ever be.'

All agog, aglow with such pleasure that I didn't stop to ask myself what she might really mean, I was determined to be even *more* interesting. I paid the bill, and afterwards, waiting to hail a black cab on the King's Road, asked her to sleep with me.

'No,' she said, not matter-of-factly and not quite gently either. I was hooked.

Whereas Janie, like myself, came from sections of the middle class whose indeterminacy could disguise any amount of dysfunction and even, in the case of my own family, crime, Chrissie was definitely, assertively, what my father would have called a 'nob'. The next time we met, when she went to the ladies', I searched through that leather satchel she took with her everywhere. I didn't imagine there'd be a sonnet she was working up on my behalf. There was a purse, a notepad, a pair of tights still sheathed in Cellophane, a lipstick, and – here was a surprise – Bertrand Russell's *Introduction to Philosophy*, the Allen & Unwin paperback. Her handwriting was like my stepsister's, a chorus line of bubbles, standard issue for the English public school girl. There was a cheque-book with her full name printed: The Hon. Chrissie Scott-Willoughby.

Honourable. How did one get to be an 'honourable'? Pete wasn't, so far as I knew. Did that mean her father was Lord X or even the Earl of Somewhere?

'Tell me about your parents,' I said.

'Oh, they're not very interesting,' she said. 'Daddy was in the RAF, but not during the war. He never flew in combat. My mother's just my mother, I suppose. She knows people at the *Guardian*. They might be able to help you.'

She was fuzzy about other areas of her life as well. I gathered she had a flat, owned a flat, down in Fulham, but she preferred to camp out with friends. She seemed intriguingly estranged from the very stratum of society of which she was such obvious offspring. In that we were alike, on the run – or so I told myself. She was twenty-four.

'You know what I think?' she said. 'You should be more curious about other people.'

I almost told her about the satchel. I said, 'I'm curious about you, aren't I?'

Chrissie lit up a Marlboro.

If I thought Pete knew London nothing prepared me for her. Wherever we went people rushed forward to kiss Chrissie on both cheeks. King's Road shops let her take clothes on tick. She knew where to get a dress at ten at night or a free packet of Marlboro any time, from a little booth on Old Compton Street. She knew pubs, clubs, and *maître d*'s swept open their arms as if they were lovers. I mushroomed in their estimation because she was on my arm. At L'Ecu de France, Rules, San Gennaro, Joe Allen, I learned about London as surely as I was finding my way around a wine list.

Soon I was in love with her and the surprising things that happened, the opportunities that rose up by magic. Cabs materialized out of nowhere when she needed them. We were in Sir John Soane's Museum, looking at Hogarth's cycle *The Rake's Progress*, when a man in baggy corduroy trousers came up, pressed upon her two tickets for the opera that night, raised his hands as if she were the one who deserved thanks, and walked away without aword.

She could be rude and tough. Drink appeared not to affect her at all. She had little sense of humour but a fretful appetitite for scandal and gossip and when I couldn't offer titbits about other people or books I gave her myself, my own family history. In return she gave me the number of a friend of her mother's, a producer for the BBC who was starting up a new radio programme – comedy. They needed writers and/or performers. I went for an interview, an audition the day after that, and was back a week later for a run-through. One of the other contributors, a middle-aged media doctor with mad hair and a spotted yellow bow-tie, turned to me with a grin: 'Well, there's no doubt who's the *star*.' I was so thrilled I accidentally took the lift down to the basement where I got lost in a maze of dingy grey-carpeted corridors and locked studios with the red recording lights off. When I called the producer as arranged it was bad news. The brass at the BBC had decided not to go ahead, she was very sorry, but since I was a friend of Chrissie's mother she put me in touch with someone else, a fellow with one of the local radio stations, a laid-back hippie who needed a film reviewer for his programme. 'Need a guy with a shovel,' he said. 'To heave some heavy cultural snow. Or is that shit?' I watched Fellini's *Casanova* in an otherwise empty theatre off Leicester Square. Donald Sutherland traversed a lagoon of heaving black plastic, and I wrote my review on the upper deck of a number 9 bus sailing back to Hammersmith. I kept the sentences short and enjoyed myself in front of the microphone, waving my hands a lot. There was a sticky moment when the presenter asked for a comparison with Fellini's earlier work, of which I'd only seen *Juliet of the Spirits*, tanked up with Tony late one night at the Cambridge Arts Theatre. But I had a shovel. I heaved whatever it was. I ill-advisedly used the word 'fuck' on air and was none the less, or perhaps because of that, invited back the next week, to talk about the new Philip Roth novel, *The Professor of Desire*, which I'd also been able to bag for review at *Time Out*. Waiting at a desk littered with plastic cups and filled ashtrays, I found a box full of index cards, notes kept on contributors. 'SMILES A LOT,' I read of my previous appearance. 'BRIGHT. BEWARE OF OBSCENITIES. UNBALANCED?' The ghost of Kafka was there, stalking the BBC in faded Levi's, desert boots, and with a VW van parked outside.

*

The Blue Suit

I was travelling between two modes of thinking again. This time it was Chrissie on the one side and everything else on the other, which included work, family, my room at Mrs Peters's, and a certain amount of crime. I wasn't earning enough to support myself, let alone the life I was leading with her. I thought I always had to pretend to be flush. I didn't see other friends. I took the pieces of stolen jewellery and silverware and sold them at the shops on High Holborn. There were others besides the one owned by the man with the bow-tie. I got used to the idea that I was going to be depressed and shocked by how little money I was offered for these items, though the pearl necklace kept me going for a few weeks. By now my bank account was so deep in the red that my own cheque-book and credit card had been reclaimed by the bank, and any money I paid in was immediately set against the overdraft. I visited the accounts departments at *Time Out*, *New Society*, and the BBC, and asked to be paid in cash. This was highly irregular, but they went along.

I bought or stole first editions, and sold some of them on. Ike, one of the young crowd who worked at 84 Charing Cross Road, an *émigré* from Hong Kong with aviator glasses and a smile more or less permanently splitting in half his smooth round face, pointed out to me that if I wished to become of more value selling books I should find more valuable books to sell. This utterance was as mysterious to me as Confucius. I found myself thinking about Tahlia, the house in Knightsbridge, her grandfather's little Renoir. The problem wouldn't be the getting of the thing, but its disposal. There'd been a story about a pair of Van Goghs stolen from a gallery in Amsterdam which had reappeared three weeks later, neatly diapered in burlap sacks and sitting on the boards of a farmer's cart. The thieves simply hadn't known what to do with them. If, say, there were a career pyramid for crime, like working one's way up through IBM, I needed a teacher. When I wasn't with Chrissie I seemed to live almost outside consciousness, in a mysterious torpor. This torpor never really left me. Stuck with my novel, I packed up the first hundred pages into an envelope and posted them to Guillermo, certain that he'd love what I'd done, and hoping that a few words from him would free my block and help me fly through the rest.

When Chrissie confessed to me, a little sheepishly, that she'd been thinking about going to university, to read philosophy, we caught the train to Cambridge where I took her to tea with my old tutor, the horse-faced dean and disbeliever in the literal truth of the Resurrection. 'Metaphysics, mmm,' he said, beaming at us over a cup of Darjeeling, and gave Chrissie the low-down on what to expect if she were to be successful in her application to study as a mature student. 'Something of an adolescent obsession I've always felt, whether the world is real or not, whether there is such a thing as external reality. We do have to move on from that. Logic is what causes most bother. It's quite hard to catch hold of unless you have some background in mathematics.'

He stretched out his legs, balanced one vast brown brogue on top of the other, and examined the resulting steeple of leather with a little satisfied grunt. He smiled at Chrissie, who sat up straight with her knees pressed together, and then his eyes travelled across the room to me. The penny dropped, for both of us: until this moment he'd not had the faintest who I was.

'Except for Mr . . .'

'Rayner.'

'Except for Mr Rayner here, of course, who kept having trouble with *ethics* I seemed to remember.' He exploded with that same nervous gust of laughter.

On the way out, while he was shepherding Chrissie through the oak outer doors, I spotted a book on a shelf, and, with two nimble steps, a quick grab, netted it beneath my jacket. 'Lovely to see you again, sir.'

On the train back to London I presented Chrissie with the book, a hardback of Wittgenstein's *Philosophical Investigations*. 'Interesting stuff,' I said.

'Did you steal this?'

I was featureless. I felt a little prickle of excitement. I told her of course not.

She stared for a moment, then shrugged and yawned. That night I asked her again to sleep with me and when she again said no, every bit as firmly as before, I more or less had another of my tantrums.

'Fuck you!'

'I wish you would,' she bafflingly said.

'That's it,' I said. 'I don't want to see you again.'

'You *are* extraordinary,' she said. 'Grow up.'

*

Around this time my father came south to live in London. We met one night in Covent Garden at a pub where the stripped and unvarnished floorboards were sprinkled with sawdust and the bright tinkle of a player-piano came from near the door. He was waiting, already at a table, when I arrived, and though he was dressed as usual in navy blazer, grey slacks, and black slip-on shoes, he looked very different, pale and tired, with a nervous tic pulsing under his left eye. He seemed to have shrunk.

Connie had died, and her sons had kicked him out immediately after the funeral. 'Gave me the bum's rush,' he said. 'Wouldn't let me take the car, my suits, not even a clean shirt.' He threw back his head, blinked, and flicked his eyes upwards with a sardonic little roll, a gesture I hadn't seen in more than ten years but so immediately recognizable and characteristic I felt it in my bones and wanted to cry. I'd seen it a hundred times, his shut-eye shrug at the world.

He was christened John Bertram Rayner, but was always called Jack, Flash Jack, Black Jack, Jack the Lad. For a while he had a younger sister, Joan, but she died when he was six and she herself only three or so. This was in the 1920s, and, after that, despite all of his mother's fears, he roamed Bradford at will, hunting for treasure in the snow, or hiding out on his own to go to the flicks at Saltaire where one of the cashiers, tired of trying to stop him sneaking in, wrote out a ticket that said he could come whenever he wanted – for free, and he didn't have to hide.

The Blue Suit

All his life – and against increasing odds, ever more insistent claims from reality – he accepted the possibility of such a blessing, the ticket that would make swift amends for any misfortune or misdemeanour. He was superstitious, as I am, and believed in chance and magic more than he ever let on, and certainly more than was wise. Ever hopeful that the nag he'd backed would come in at 50–1, he didn't let himself get down in the dumps for too long, although that night at the pub in Covent Garden, after Connie's death, he seemed to have taken a blow from which he'd never recover.

He told me he was staying at a servicemen's club across the river on the other side of Waterloo Bridge. He'd been looking for a job, without any luck so far. Meanwhile he'd been tramping the streets, hour after hour, not knowing where his feet were taking him. He was sad and confused, in trouble. 'She was a lady, wasn't she?' he said. 'Took me on, no questions asked. She was a lovely lady.' He drank and set down his glass with tremendous care. 'You liked her too, didn't you, son?'

My father was reaching out. I wanted to be his friend, in a blurry way, to comfort him, but I wanted no part of his future. I didn't think I hated him, but I did. 'Yes, Dad, I did. I liked her a lot,' I said, true words not truly felt; they served their purpose – they got me off the hook. I tried to make him laugh by telling him about Chrissie. 'She's an honourable,' I said. 'The daughter of a lord or something. Imagine.' I bought us drink after drink until I didn't feel anything and I hoped he couldn't either.

163

At the end of the evening he hugged me and gave me a sloppy kiss. 'Let's keep in touch then, eh, Rich?' I promised that we would. I promised that I'd call him in a couple of days. It was two years before we spoke or met again.

I think one of the reasons I lied so much at this time was that I didn't think anything had happened to me. I'd suppressed my family history so routinely and for so long that it didn't seem to count; I'd lied so often I'd lost sight of where the true lines were, and, when confronted with traces, I didn't know what to be. I stumbled away, regrouped, imagined I could just cruise on. In my room at Mrs Peters's I sat down on the little folding wooden chair in front of my typewriter, fingered the keys, and unexpectedly started to sob.

I made good on my threat never to see Chrissie again for all of one very bad week, and then I wrote her a letter, or rather cribbed one, from S. J. Perelman's salty portrait of working in Hollywood. I didn't tell her that I missed her and I certainly didn't tell her that I didn't care whether she slept with me or not. I told her how in the *Time Out* office there was an enormous funeral pyre composed of defunct Labour Party manifestos – not revolutionary enough. There was the crisp tang of a frying reviewer (this one) who'd dared announce that he thought Evelyn Waugh's *Vile Bodies* the funniest book of the century. Meanwhile upstairs at the news desk one of the reporters, he had yellow eyes and a beard like a loony prophet, had hired a hit man to fly in from Detroit and take out Margaret Thatcher. This had been voted upon during an editorial meeting.

We took a taxi to a house in Chelsea, a mews somewhere to the north of Sloane Square. It was a private club. There was a man at the door, a bouncer in a black tuxedo; another stood in the hall beneath a chandelier. To the left, in the drawing-room, people weren't talking much. They were gambling. Backgammon boards had been set up on tables. Dice clicked and rattled, tumbling from leather cups. Beyond that the library was a small-scale casino with two roulette wheels where the serious stuff was going on.

She offhandedly introduced me to someone called Michael and disappeared. Michael was tall and skinny and he wore his hair unfashionably long. The cheeks on his wide face were polished and pink, but not healthy; they looked like melting wax. He had a grave, dissolute manner. It was only when he smiled, and lines inscribed themselves down those cheeks and at the corners of his eyes, that his face changed, became that of a charmer. 'Do you like the Sex Pistols? Do you think *Margaret Thatcher* likes the Sex Pistols?' he asked. 'Of course I *never* play roulette. Never get excited, never lose my head, never win. I'm just an unlucky boy.'

During my spree I'd gambled at Cambridge, on the horses, 'the ponies' as my father called them. Once I'd made a modest score and had felt very grown-up as the bookie counted out a pile of used tenners and other punters looked enviously on. What theatre, what optimism – to dream that a bet could make everything right, could reclaim the beginning of the beginning.

Michael didn't egg me on. When I went out with Chrissie I tried to make sure I had quite a bit of cash in my pocket. I took it out now and lost all of it – over a hundred pounds – on two or three spins of the wheel. A stranger stared at me from the other side of the baize when he saw that I'd stopped. 'What's the matter?' he said. 'Too heavy for you?'

This made some sort of a bond between Michael and me. 'Why do you want to be a writer?' he asked.

'My stepfather's a writer,' I said, another thing I hadn't quite put together before. I'd seen his name in print and the fantasy had sprung from there, associated in my mind with cricket, holidays on the Med, and three-piece suits of best Bradford wool, the best in the world – as well as the books I loved.

I left Michael to look for Chrissie, and strolled through some of the other rooms. There was more gambling, a room with a fire in the grate, and lots of people talking and laughing in shrill voices; there were even a few punks who'd found their way in, and were sipping cans of lager, as if a little cowed by the surroundings, but there was no sign of Chrissie. Michael was in the kitchen, behaving as though he owned the place, or didn't care who did. From his pocket he pulled out a syringe, all crackly in its Cellophane wrapper. There was a hiss, and then a pop as he lit one of the gas rings on the oven. He melted some crystals in a spoon, diluted the molten liquid with a little water, and drew back the plunger of the syringe so the liquid was sucked up. He took off his jacket and tie, rolled up his sleeve, and deftly knotted the tie around his upper arm, jerking it tight with his teeth. He found a vein, and injecting himself, let out a little sigh.

I tried to maintain an appearance of cool. A trickle of thick blood chased the needle out of the vein and, gaining weight, rolled round the corner of Michael's forearm and dripped on to the floor. I thought I was going to faint.

The grinning man who'd sneered at me over the roulette table had followed us down and was standing at the door.

Michael offered the syringe, which was still half-full, a red filter of blood mingled with heroin. A drop of blood was poised at the end of the needle. The other fellow went a little green. 'What's the matter?' said Michael. 'Too heavy for you?'

Michael, I was to learn from Chrissie two or three days later, was Chrissie's husband, her *estranged* husband; they were getting a divorce, or she thought so – really she didn't know quite what was going on. Once I'd got over the immediate shock, and the certainty that I'd have to run away back to Yorkshire to get out of the situation (I didn't see that there was no situation, as far as she was concerned), this didn't make me unhappy or uneasy, as it should have. On the contrary it seemed to help explain a number of things – such as why she refused to go to bed with me; it added to her glamour and thus mine as well, I thought. I was involved with a married aristocrat. This was life with unexpected twists; this was what I'd been waiting for.

One night I had to go and pick her up when she'd been arrested for drunk-driving. I got to see the other side of Tottenham Court Road Police Station, the front office. A young constable gave us a lift and on the way back Chrissie made both of us wait in the car while she popped out on an errand, picking up Michael's drugs, as it turned out. Oh, great. I didn't get it. There was no one to spare my poor, slow mind: this was the kind of thing that kept her going.

Afterwards we talked, or rather she did, starting slowly but soon picking up pace as she launched into an elaborate incantation of the many ways in which Michael pissed her off. He lied, he stole, he was always late, when he bothered to show up at all. He insulted her friends and thought he could make it up by being especially kind to her family. He had her running all over London for drugs. He'd been in rehab five times, or was it six now? The last time, as part of the therapy, they'd made him take a job at McDonald's, where he'd been fired for doling out Big Macs free to pensioners. There'd been a clinic in Scotland, and before that, one in New York. Michael was getting to know all the expensive clinics of the world. Meanwhile he went on with the lies, the stealing, the smiling and being charming as if the world were duty bound to adore him.

'He's impossible to live with, and so I don't. He's a fucking junkie.' She was afraid, she said, stabbing out her cigarette, that he'd drag her down with him, all the way to the bottom. The worst of it was that she couldn't get away. She knew she should, but couldn't because she couldn't help believing that if only she went that one step further, gave him that little extra shove, he'd change, she'd save him and everything would be roses again. 'Bloody stupid, wouldn't you say? Bloody maddening too.'

Chrissie had broken suddenly and violently into song, and I thought I was lucky to have fallen in with someone so glamorous and unstable. I remembered Pete and the fuss he'd made about buying that suit of bottle-green velvet, the arguing with his sisters, the phone call to the shop, the dizzy cab ride to the hushed lobby of the Ritz for an envelope stuffed with cash. Everything about the rich seemed to involve insouciance and danger, lots of noise. They pretended not to care, and maybe they really didn't, but not caring was always conducted at high volume.

It had been a while now and I hadn't heard from Guillermo about the first half of my novel, so I called and he agreed that I should go to his flat to talk about it. He was dapper and impish and precise, as before, but dressed this time in a grey double-breasted suit. As Miriam handed me a small cup of espresso I sat back and waited for the liberating words of praise.

'This,' Guillermo said, 'is one of the most unusual things that has come my way for some time.'

Of course it is, I thought, and sipped at the espresso.

'It is, fundamentally, a mistake. I see that you've put in an enormous effort, and it's not badly written, but I'm afraid it won't do. It's worse than mediocre. It's not a bad novel, simply, it's not a novel at all. It's artificial with no artifice to make it seem real.'

I felt my face set into its *rigor mortis* grin.

He went on, 'I am very sorry to be so brutal but I hope I can save you time by persuading you not to go on with this. Please don't try to mark with an asterisk and salvage anything. Throw it all away and try again. Then throw that away and try again.'

I tried to protest – surely there was something.

'It is dull,' he said. 'Now let's talk about Buñuel.'

I felt as though a hundred bandits were trying to annihilate me with knives. I was sure he couldn't be right. The book was good, I knew, even though I'd been having problems with it.

In my room, I looked over the pages and saw all of a sudden that the tone was phony, the character's situation no longer interesting or true; I'd dropped down a mine-shaft and he was still at the top, waving with a desperation he hoped was aplomb. I didn't believe him any more. I tried to convince myself that perhaps I'd feel this way only about the one particular passage, but, having made myself a cup of tea and scanned back over the rest of it, I felt the dead empty weight of every page.

I'd pinned so much on this, even though over the months I'd been forced to make concessionary adjustments. First there'd been the promise to finish and sell the book by Christmas. I'd had to abandon that. Next had come the feeling – more realistic, or so I thought – that it would be OK to publish by the end of my twenty-second year. Now I saw, not only the impossibility of even this diminished objective, but the very real chance that I'd never finish a book at all. To start another – get it right – could take years, even if I had an idea for one, which I didn't. I didn't know where to go. Oddly again, I wasn't too bothered, I felt floppy and relaxed, optimistic, certain something would turn up. I didn't think I need ask anyone's help or advice.

I was riding the Underground when I felt a migraine coming on. The Tube map above the head of the fellow sitting opposite seemed suddenly garish and brilliant. Its lines of red, yellow and blue seemed to bulge and glow, as if they were neon, alive. The compartment was so crowded and stuffy that I started to sweat and by the time I stumbled off the train at King's Cross I was already in the haze. Outside the station a ray of low winter sunlight bounced off a car windshield and shot straight into my eye like an arrow. My vision started to wobble and shiver.

I bought a Coke, swilled back some of my tablets, and leaned against a wall with my eyes shut. Ten minutes later it was no longer as if a knife were twisting in my brain. I felt light and woolly-headed – the Migril did that.

When I'd been in this state as a teenager, a friend had

once asked me what day of the week it was. He'd asked me five times in quick succession and I'd given a different answer each time. It was like having a concussion, except that, once the drugs had kicked in, there was no pain – the sensation was of a bee buzzing far away inside my head. Its sting caused only pins and needles, almost delicious tinglings at the ends of my fingers and toes.

At this stage the best thing was always to go home and sleep it off. Instead I broke into a house, a smart-looking place in Islington at the end of a terrace with a passage running down the side. It reminded me of the house where I'd met Tahlia. In my mind it became not only the house where I'd met her, but also the one which contained the little Renoir her grandparents had.

I broke in at the back, on the paved stone patio, through french windows painted white. In the centre of the room I found myself in there was a desk with a red leather top and a chair behind it, facing out. I turned back to see the view: a lawn, two or three apple trees, pruned rose bushes, a wall of sooty brick.

Book shelves lined the wall behind the desk. To my left, pictures on the wall, modern, not very good. I was an art critic now. To my right a sofa with a Laura Ashley pattern and a wooden chair set plumb in front, as if someone had been reading on the sofa with his or her feet up. There was a wine glass on the floor with a dab of scarlet in the bottom, dried-up dregs. I was looking at my feet and the polished, even, stripped-pine floorboards. I didn't seem to be able to connect these impressions

or deduce anything from them. I was disattached from
the physical world – but every now and then it would
shoot out a wire to hook my eye and remind me it was
there. First a polished brass coal scuttle reeled me in, then
a blue vase without flowers, now a paper clip stuck to the
edge of the desk with a drawing pin. I was jerked towards
these objects, seeing one and then another with a shock. It
was hard to believe that if I looked away from one it
would be there when I looked back. My eye made jump
cuts.

I knew I shouldn't be doing this, but now I had a strong
idea that the house contained not only Tahlia's Renoir but
was also filled with expensive telescopes and cameras,
solid silver cutlery. In the migraine haze I'd now mixed in
a story a friend had told me about a visit he'd made to his
landlord who had been sitting in a high-backed chair
counting gold coins. I imagined the coins were here too. I
only had to find them.

I was puzzled why I couldn't find what I was looking
for. Everything had such a luminous appearance, each
object was so sharp and discrete, that all seemed equally
wonderful. Once or twice I'd tried to write while I'd been
suffering an attack only to discover that sentences, lucid
and logical at the time, revealed themselves afterwards as
scrambled gibberish, written in some migraine code for
which the waking self no longer had a key. So it was now.
A red plastic pencil sharpener I found on the desk struck
me as of quite extraordinary value; I picked it up, admired,
dropped it in my bag. After that I collected a Shaeffer

ballpen and an Elton John cassette, delighted as if they were krugerrands.

The carpets had been taken up in the room on the other side of the hallway. It was being redecorated. Floors and furniture were draped with tatty white sheets and a sweet smell rose from opened bags of plaster. There were two stepladders with a plank making a bridge between them so the workmen could get at the ceiling. A far section of the wall, to the left of the fireplace, hadn't been finished yet; there was a gap of about two feet by a foot and a half with bare wood webbing visible at the back. It occurred to me that I should plaster this little section of wall. This seemed a startling illumination.

I went to the back of the house, to the kitchen, to get some water. I stuck my head under the other tap as the bucket was filling and pressed water into my eyes and against the back of my neck. Cold drops ran under my collar and down my spine in a delicious trickle.

Two types of plaster are used. First there's the filling, thick brown stuff which is to be applied clumsily and smoothed over. Then there's the next coat, the finish, which has to be mixed to the consistency of double cream and put on as fast as possible. Here's where the art is: no bumps and ridges must show. It's an immensely satisfying job when it goes right, broad sweeps creating a light grey surface level as the trowel itself. Tricky on an entire wall, but for a small area like this – 'Easy as sticking stamps,' the plasterer in Yorkshire had said, 'get 'em done wi' a couple o' licks.'

The plaster squelched and swished as I moved the trowel, sweeping in one direction only. On the third or fourth stroke I remembered where I was. I dropped the trowel, went back into the study, and collected my bag. I escaped the house, my hands gloved in thin grey plaster.

Later, in my room at Mrs Peters's, I inspected the Sheaffer pen and the Elton John cassette tape as if they were, not krugerrands, but curiosities from some archaeological dig. I couldn't believe what I'd done. The episode seemed bizarre and dreamlike, yet here was the evidence, sitting on the desk next to my typewriter, all the more baffling because so concrete.

It seemed quite funny, given that I'd got away with it, but then, as if I were a scientist pouring one chemical into another to produce a yet more violent reaction, I remembered that I hadn't been wearing gloves. I must have left my fingerprints all over the place, and the police had those now, as well as my address, filed on index card or computer. Perhaps the Flying Squad would have been called in. It seemed to be par for the course. 'Yeah,' the Sweeney guy would say. 'All the unmistakable signs. He's at it again. The Cambridge philosophy graduate.' It was serious this time. There seemed no reason why I wouldn't be caught – all they had to do was put the bits of very obvious evidence together. I went all liquid again. I felt sick.

*

That night I couldn't sleep. I went for a walk. I stood on Hammersmith Bridge at three in the morning and contemplated suicide. Really I knew there was no question of that. The following morning I thought I'd better leave Mrs Peters's, so at least they'd have to track me down, but this course of action seemed, after a couple of hours, too difficult and complicated. Where would I go?

I phoned Scotland Yard. I did this in the same spirit as I'd been chasing Chrissie, certain it was the wrong thing to do, unable to help myself. I thought I was very smooth. I introduced myself as a journalist and before I could say anything else the woman on the switchboard transferred me to press relations where a man answered, Sergeant Brand.

I realized I was expected to have a name. 'I'm Richard Page,' I said, trying to sound bright and purposeful. 'I work for the *New Statesman*.'

This was dumb, I knew as soon as the words were out, because for a Scotland Yard official the word 'new' combined with 'statesman' meant only one thing: lefty rag, digging dirt. At *Time Out* there happened to be two reporters named Duncan Campbell. One had the (I imagined) good fortune to live with the actress Julie Christie, the other also did work for the *New Statesman* and was expert in the legal and illegal ways in which the Government gathered information concerning individuals. They were known as Duncan Zhivago and Duncan Secrets. A recent article by Duncan Secrets had been the unconscious prompting of the scheme to call Scotland Yard. This same article now caused Sergeant Brand's voice to rise like the rate of inflation: 'The *New Statesman*. Yes?'

I tried to make amends. I had a sudden desire to be exceptionally pleasant. I said I didn't want to do the usual sort of thing, but a sympathetic piece, something that would take the police's side for once. About fingerprint techniques. My ad lib grew wings. About fingerprint techniques and how efficient they were these days. Perhaps he could give me some idea. Was the system so efficient now that all prints could be checked against those on record? A few case histories might be interesting, I said, to give an example or two where modern methods had led to speedy capture and arrest. And just how speedy was that? Were we talking days or weeks? *Hours*. Hmmmm?

I hung up.

In a flop sweat I pressed my forehead against the wall. For a moment I even imagined that Sergeant Brand might have a monitor screen on his desk that could trace phone calls such as this one. With agonizing effort, slowly, I calmed myself down. Everything I'd stolen from the house had been worthless. Perhaps the break-in hadn't been reported. Even if it had the house might not have been dusted for prints. Or the prints might be smudged. And their methods might not be so hot after all. Blurry hopes, but soothing.

The fever came back that night and I took the tube to the Victoria Embankment. The Thames was a dark blank, puddled with milky reflected light. I walked for a while with my head down before forcing myself to stare up at

Richard Rayner

New Scotland Yard, a pink but otherwise ominously characterless structure. Most of the ten or twelve floors had lights on – detectives working late, or so I imagined. The place was pent up on the edge of the river like a warship.

After a day or two my funk blew away, leaving me clear and ready again for anything. I was an idiot, but I had reserves of courage and optimism that amaze me now.

Ten

Chrissie phoned to say she and Michael were planning a
trip. 'Up north,' she said, as if this were the Arctic Circle
we were talking about. 'Yorkshire.'

I shut my eyes, supposing this was it, the big boot.
Inevitable: Michael with all his problems made a more
enticing proposition, and he'd been to Eton. He had the
Establishment and centuries of barking mad aristo tra-
dition on his side. I was afraid I'd cry.

'I was hoping you'd come as well,' she said, hesitating a
little, as if I might say no.

She drove with a casual expertise I'd thought special to
my father, legs apart, hands in lap, fingers resting lightly
on the bottom of the wheel. Michael sat up front in the
passenger seat, and I was in the back. When 'Night Fever'
by the Bee Gees came on the radio we all sang along, and
he and I thrust our hands in the air like John Travolta. We
stopped at a service station south of Sheffield where
Chrissie and Michael made not unfriendly jokes about *oop
north* and the doubtless extraordinary customs of its

inhabitants. I told them about Nanna Windhill who drank two bottles of Mackeson stout each night, for her health, and used this as excuse never to go to the doctor because surgery hours clashed with *Coronation Street*, her favourite TV soap, whose characters were every bit as real to her as I, her own flesh and blood. She watched with Mackeson in one hand and a bag of mints beside her to the accompaniment of a gentle creaking from below, because she hid the newspapers under the cushion of her chair so my grandfather couldn't get at them.

They both laughed. Michael's eyes were big as he said, 'No,' extending the word until it was several ohs long; I knew I shouldn't have been so pleased with myself. It was cheap. They weren't telling stories about their families.

Michael excused himself to go to the toilets at the back of the cafeteria and I summoned up the courage to ask Chrissie what was going on. I managed to find, not so much the wrong words, as precisely the wrong pushy tone, and she shrugged, saying, 'Aren't you glad?' I settled back into myself, fiddling with the tomato-shaped ketchup dispenser, waiting around to be acted upon. Chrissie tapped a cigarette out of her Marlboro packet. On one finger there were angry red sores around the nail where she'd been picking at the cuticle. She lit up.

'I love you,' I said, and even as the words came out they felt insincere, as when I'd asked Janie to marry me. It was just that the moment had seemed to call for them, so I delivered up, on cue.

Chrissie's face softened none the less. 'I'm not sure that

you do,' she said in a soft voice, and gazed out the window at the headlights swishing by. Square bubbles of light reached out above the lanes of traffic where a bridge led to an identical cafeteria on the other side.

I saw Michael coming back, taking a slow, weaving course, kicking up his feet with giant steps. His pale eyes were shiny and clear. He sat back down with a huge pantomime grin, picked up a chip and threw it at Chrissie. A second came at me, smearing grease on my cheek. 'I'm moonwalking,' he said. One more chip, right in Chrissie's face. 'I'm stoned.'

He said that when he was stoned he lost heaven and earth. He forgot that he existed at all, and at that moment his joy was very glad indeed. 'Richard's smiling. But then he's always smiling, isn't he?' He closed one hand into a fist and reached out across the table to rap me on the forehead with it. 'Who's in here? What dashing dunce of dreams?'

I felt myself die a little, and Chrissie got up to go.

'Don't,' he said, almost desperately, his mood changed at once. Too late: Chrissie was already halfway across the cafeteria, that shabby black leather satchel shouldered like a weapon.

Michael was exhausted all of a sudden. There were marks under his eyes, almost like scars, swollen black half-moons. His blond hair flopped on to the plate, trailing through chip fat and tomato ketchup. He apologized. 'Don't mind me,' he said. 'Fiddledy-dee.'

He asked if Chrissie and I were sleeping together. He

smiled when he asked this, and I felt myself die a little more. 'Are you fucking my wife?'

It was odd: until this moment I hadn't quite accepted the fact of their marriage. To be married was to be like my mother and stepfather. I'd never thought of my mother and father as being married either, but then, in the time that I'd known them, they hadn't been. 'No,' I said, shocked out of myself.

Back in the car Michael sang, made jokes, and fell asleep; he snored like a B-52, woke up again, and sang some more. 'You're the one that I love – *ooo! ooo! ooo!*' Chrissie kept the speed up to ninety, and I fell asleep myself, a trick I'd perfected on all those excrutiating journeys through the Scottish highlands with Janie and her parents.

When I woke up the car was so smoky and hot I had a headache, and Michael was putting on another great performance, flapping about with maps and bits of paper. 'Micklethwaite Road,' he said. 'That's what we're after. Micklethwaite Road. Must be where Michael Caine comes from. And all the time I thought he was a Londoner.'

Chrissie and Michael were planning a crime of their own, as it turned out. They had two stolen cheque-books with them, and their scheme was to forge a cheque for fifteen thousand pounds, use this to open an account, get a few temporary cheques, and then the next day go to a branch of the same bank in a nearby town and try to cash one of those, not for the whole amount, but a largish sum, say eight or nine hundred, before the first had bounced.

They'd done this three or four times now, and there'd been a hitch the last time so Michael had decided it would be safer with someone outside in the car, just in case. And since I didn't drive, and the bank routine rather depended on having two people, he thought that Chrissie and I would go in together, posing as a couple.

Chrissie told me about this the next day. It was a brisk early April morning. We were in Littleborough, a small town with a wool exchange like a monolith at its centre, a square sandstone building whose clumpy tower was stained black by soot. All the other buildings were dwarfed by their natural surroundings. Moorland hills rose on either side, glimmering and seeming to change in shape with the cloud-shadows that raced across.

I wasn't surprised. At least everything was clear: they were using me, and here was Chrissie offering me a chance not to go along with it, if I didn't want to. One moment it was sunny; there was a flurry of rain the next. A fierce wind blew. At last it was spring; an old woman stood quite still in the street with brilliant yellow shopping bags in either hand. She had one of those disappointed soufflés for a hat and, waddling along, she seemed dazed and off balance, until a sudden gust made her reach up to her head to prevent the hat flying off, an action she performed with surprising grace. Littleborough had an atmosphere as if it really did have to hide down and crouch, otherwise the town and its entire population would be whirled away.

Chrissie and I climbed up on to the moors. It was a battle against the wind until we reached the top and there was Littleborough, far below, with a background of brown and purple moors, rising and sweeping away even higher than the wool exchange. There was the spire of a church I hadn't noticed before, and, behind that, a graveyard, full of squat black tombstones. All around there were the same sinuous wave-like hills, the scoops into which they fell only revealing other hills beyond, crowned with wild bleak moor.

She said that Michael was taking care of the trickiest bit even as we spoke – opening the account. That really required a performance, she said. His story was that he was a London antique dealer, planning a new business in the area.

The whole scheme sounded pretty harebrained, but then who was I to say?

Michael would make an arrangement with the first bank so we could take money out at the second. Of course Bank 2 would ring up Bank 1 and the big hope was that Bank 1 wouldn't have made a note of the fact that the cheque was still in clearing. The account would just say that so much was available. If they had, everything depended on bluff. Bank 2 couldn't possibly know that the original cheque was forged.

'Not that it matters,' she said in a languid voice, 'since you're not going to do it.'

'Oh, I'll do it,' I said, staring at her profile, and she turned to me with an expression of surprise.

She smiled. She said that once, during a dinner at someone else's house, Michael had excused himself. Ten minutes later she began to worry about where he was. She found him in the bedroom, curled up in a chair with a bottle of green Chartreuse and an emptied bottle of sleeping pills. An ambulance had taken them both to hospital. For a while the doctors didn't think he'd pull through. Chrissie sat on a bench in the waiting room and started to cry. She couldn't stop – it was as if someone had turned on a tap. She said to herself that this was boring, she hated this, and that if he lived she'd leave him for good. She made a solemn promise to herself, a bargain if you like. It was four in the morning when a nurse came out and told her Michael was going to be all right. She found him in intensive care with tubes up his nose and an IV in his arm. He was barely conscious, but still able to say: 'Don't worry. It's just a shortcoming of the pharmaceutical industry.' She'd remembered that she liked him. She liked him more than anyone else she knew.

'And so here I am,' she said. 'I know it's stupid.'

'Re-imagine yourself. Get away. *Propel* yourself,' I said. I sounded like Werner Erhardt. 'Nobody need be anything they don't want to.'

'You don't have any earthly idea what it's like. You know nothing – about me, about him, about what we've shared together.' She shrugged, and added less sharply: 'Anyway, at least Michael doesn't mind if you laugh at him. Not like lots of men. Not like you.' She said this without malice, as if commenting on a story she'd read, an interesting discovery that minute swum into view: MEN WITHOUT HUMOUR, *featuring Richard Rayner.*

I flared up. 'You'll be fine. You'll get over this and end up married to someone rich. It's what your type is bred for.'

'I'm married to Michael.'

'He's a junkie and we both know he's not going to make it.' My voice was quite level. 'He's killing himself. He's going to die.'

The sun went in, and this change in the light turned the purple heather tawny. Chrissie was crying. She cried so quietly you didn't hear her at all. 'You shit. That's a terrible thing to say.'

'It's the truth.'

'Fuck off. Fuck off back to London.'

I looked up at the clouds whizzing towards us with their cargoes of rain. 'I'm crazy about you,' I said, meaning it now, and for once I'd tightened everything to the correct nutty pitch.

'I'm crazy about you too,' she said.

That night in the pub Michael was genial and sunny, playing pool with the locals. One moment he had the cue tucked under his arm, a baton, the next he whipped it out and wheeled the table. 'Eight ball!' he cried. He wore a black polo-neck and a black leather jacket. His hair was washed, combed so that it gleamed, and he had a little badge that said: The Stranglers. He was a little wild-eyed but cheerful.

One of the local lads stared at Chrissie with the same gooey expression I'm sure had been witnessed on my face more than a few times. Chrissie herself drank as much or more than anyone and didn't get drunk. I meanwhile fed the jukebox and danced. My partner was short, plump, with razored black hair and a safety pin through her nose. The record was 'How Deep Is Your Love', the ballad from *Saturday Night Fever*, to which she pogoed frenziedly up and down. 'Yer don't sound much like yer grew up in Bradford,' she said. With half-amused disparagement she referred to the local males as 'Tetley Bittermen', after the beer they drank. Her own name was Phyllis, she said.

'You're kidding.'

'Yer right, it's Julie,' she said. She mimicked my accent. '*Act-u-all-ay*.' I puzzled Julie a little: on the one hand she knew I wasn't like Michael and Chrissie, but then she didn't think I was like her either; she didn't know what I was.

Chrissie was up at the bar buying a round and Michael was explaining that his great-great (or was it his great-great-*great*?) grandfather had served with Wellington at Waterloo. 'That's the sort of family I came from. Not like you lot. And look what it's done for me.'

Chrissie, Michael and I were suddenly like a family ourselves, a unit. I loved the idea. I was feeling very calm and pleased with myself when Chrissie elected to shout: 'RICHARD SAYS YOU'RE GOING TO DIE.'

There was an awful moment.

'You're not going to make it, that's what he says. You're a fucking hopeless junkie.'

Michael's blue eyes were numb and dull. 'He's severe, isn't he? A man of surprises. Saying odd things, agreeing to even odder ones. Whatever will he do next. What's the plan, eh, Richard?'

I caught Chrissie's eye. 'No plans. No good at them.'

He grinned suddenly and said, 'Something else we have in common.' He took his drink from the edge of the pool table. 'Orange juice. *Mmmm*. Tastes as bright as it looks. Especially fine when diluted with a triple vodka. As for the other thing, well, I may surprise you. If not – you'll all have to weep at my funeral.'

'I'll jump up and down and lead the chorus,' said Chrissie.

'Buckets,' Michael said. 'Hankies will be required. Mark my word.' With a strut and a little brandish of the cue, he turned away.

Next morning he gave us our parts. It was another gorgeous day in Littleborough. Chrissie and I would go into the bank and I'd write the cheque while she chatted up the cashier. He'd be outside in the car. The nice point, he said, was to get into the bank as close to closing time as possible; that way a hurried cashier might let the cheque through without all the rigmarole. *The nice point* – as if everything was logic.

I went to the bookshop for a while, the owner was talking with another customer, a man in walking boots with green socks pulled up nearly to his knees.

'So you've bin away?'

'Aye. We were going to go to London. Then it were Liverpool. We got as far as Hebden Bridge. About ten miles. Read *Heart of Darkness*. It's good, isn't it?'

'Oh aye, yeah. A gripper.'

'Got Dostoevsky's *Notes from Underground*?'

'Oh aye, yeah. Quite good.'

'I read it. Then I gave it away. It were like wading through treacle.'

Back in the pub Chrissie studied the *Daily Mail*. Michael looked at me and contorted his face. We were all comically self-conscious. Crime was a tunnel down another reality. The beer glass in my hand seemed like a prop, as did the pen that Michael gave me and with which he invited me to practise his signature, or rather his own signing of the assumed name he'd given to open the account. The two of them expressed a little surprise that I did it so easily and well.

Todmorden was on the other side of the moor. There was a cobbled market square. Fruits and vegetables were piled high on the stalls beneath red and white awnings, together with shoes, T-shirts, jeans, and cheap imitation jewellery. Where Littleborough was precarious, riding the sea of the surrounding moors, Todmorden took close shelter under that which loomed most directly over. There was no steady wind, though unexpected gusts came chuting down the valley, and made the awnings pop into sudden taut sails.

As a child I'd seen my mother help out my aunt on market stalls like these, her hands protected against the cold by woollen gloves with no fingers so she could count the change. This was the England I'd grown up in: moors, rain, wind, and the harsh, slow sounds of Yorkshire accents.

The bank was on the square's northern side, furthest away from and facing the moor, up steps beneath arches to the left of an imposing town hall, an imposing erection of soot-blackened sandstone. Michael found parking right beneath, and Chrissie and I got out. With a match between my lips, like Warren Beatty in *Bonnie and Clyde*, I felt very real and very fake. I flicked the match away. Even that gesture seemed terribly self-conscious.

There was only one open cashier's window. The man behind it was middle-aged and dressed in a pale grey summer suit, perhaps only removed that morning from the dry cleaner's plastic. He was tall and spruce, with black rectangular glasses so big they kept sliding down his nose. 'An antique shop?' he said, as if the words clearly had another meaning – opium den or sex boutique.

I explained that I had an arrangement, enabling me to cash a cheque at this branch, and I made sure he saw me sign the cheque, which I pushed under the counter where his bony fingers gathered it in, turned it over, then pulled it straight with a brisk little snap. 'Nine hundred and fifty pounds?' he said, and stabbed a doubtful digit at the bridge of his spectacles.

My father had died, I said, in a faint and I hoped conciliatory Yorkshire accent. I'd have been forced to sell up, the house and everything, had it not been for my partner – Chrissie, I let him know with a nod. She'd

190

persuaded her own father to invest and now we were busy converting the ground floor of Dad's old place into the shop. 'Fingers crossed,' I said, and I did cross my fingers, and wave them at him.

Chrissie watched this performance, trying not to smile. The digital clock on the wall behind the cashiers' windows turned over another minute: 15.27. The main bank door opened and a man came in from outside bringing with him a rush of spring air and the clatter of the market. And when the door closed there was silence again. Our cashier in the grey suit stood with casual hand on hip beside a desk where a younger man, one of his colleagues, was on the phone, to the branch in Littleborough. They glanced up at us both at the same time. Their expressions were identical, quite blank.

I felt as always when committing or trying to commit a crime. On the one hand I was a zombie, stumbling through, while on the other there was a heightened aware-ness, a tingle of excitement and fear that I was again in the area where a casual mistake might come to seem dis-astrous, even fateful. This was where the action was. I had no romantic thoughts about what I was doing, but at least I felt alive.

The clock turned again, only two minutes to closing. Someone else came in from the street and then another cashier, a woman I hadn't seen before, came from behind the oak security door. She walked to the front fiddling with a bunch of keys. She was getting ready to shut up.

We'd left it too fine. Within two minutes, less, the

female cashier would lock the door and would have to unlock it before we could get out. In effect we'd be trapped. The forged cheque that Michael had paid in the previous day wouldn't have had time yet to go through the system. It couldn't have bounced. So, if we stayed, all we had to do was bluff it out. I was used to that. On the other hand I had no idea how long ago the cheque-book had been stolen. Why hadn't I asked? If it was already on a bank list, and someone in the Littleborough branch had spotted it – we were in trouble.

Our cashier regarded me with the same bland stare.

I took Chrissie's hand, whispered that we should leave, and she turned to me with a startled manic glare. For a few moments we hissed at each other like stage villains and I was more or less tugging her to the door, aware that people were giving us looks – but no one called or shouted and then we were outside, with the wind gusting in our faces. I had a clear view of the moors, but at the bottom of the steps, where the car had been parked, there was now no car, no Michael, no Michael in the car. A wind flipped and fluttered the awnings on the stalls.

We set off to search, down the steps, Chrissie going one way while I went the other. We met up on the other side of the square and still there was no sign of him.

I was calm. It didn't much matter whether Michael had planned this all along, or grown bored, or was stoned, or whether – most likely – it was an addled combination of the three. He'd gone.

I had the same shiver between the shoulders I'd felt that

afternoon when the store detectives had caught me in London. The cashier in the grey suit had come out of the bank and was looking around the market square, together with his young colleague, the one who'd been on the phone, and a policeman. The policeman wore a peaked cap, not a helmet, which meant there must be a squad car somewhere. The three of them were at the top of the town hall steps. Neither Chrissie nor I spoke.

We turned down a narrow street, round a corner, another corner, a swift succession of streets and corners. We were on a broadish street that led out of the town when I dived into a hunting and fishing shop, and bought two grey plastic smocks with hoods so we could pass for hikers. Disguises now! The whole scene was really very humorous, if it wasn't happening to you.

We skirted a council estate, scores of grey shingle houses identical to those I'd helped rebuild, then looped back around the town. There was thunder, I think, or it might have been a huge clank of metal as several market stalls came down together. We walked past the railway station, up an alley with bulging flintstone walls, then a narrow path which took us towards the moor. It was a long climb to the crest of the hill. No one followed. After that, on the darkening bushless moor, we ran down towards Little-borough and the Wool Exchange.

Michael had skipped town. Chrissie was angry rather than surprised, evidently well used to this sort of thing. She chewed at her nails and smoked a lot. We caught a bus, where she sat with her knees bunched up against the seat-back, and, from Leeds, a train to London. At Leeds she made a phone call and found that Michael had already been in touch with her mother. He'd been in Todmorden and Littleborough looking for us all over – or so he'd said. I didn't believe that, but when Chrissie refused to discuss it, I didn't push the point. Instead I made up a story about my father. Once – in Brazil, in the suburbs of Rio – he'd got into a tangle himself over a dud cheque trying to buy a car. There came a moment when he saw that the Brazilian lads in the car showroom weren't going to fall for it. His motto? In doubt, get out. Unfortunately, on this occasion, he'd made the mistake of sporting a white suit, like Dirk Bogarde in *Death in Venice*. Two fellows from the garage, beefy mechanic types, were able to track him easily through the streets. They broke his nose, knocked loose a couple of teeth. The suit was ruined.

She said, 'You told me you'd never spoken to your father about what he did while he was away.'

'A little,' I lied. I was still trying to impress her. She was tired, and by the time I came back from the buffet car with bacon sandwiches and whisky miniatures, small double-shot bottles, light artillery, she was asleep. I leaned over and kissed her on the lips, but she didn't stir until Peterborough, when the train stopped and she dashed down the platform to make another phone call, to her mother again, to make sure that Michael was all right and to pass on the message that he shouldn't worry about her.

She'd see him back in London. Then she curled up in her seat and went back to sleep again. I should have been talking to her, at least trying, but instead I got up for the last call at the buffet. Dancing disgracefully down the carriage, wondering when my life would at last begin, I was drunk when I came back. The train scattered bright lights all over Hertfordshire and Middlesex and I wanted someone to love me the way she did him – not blindly, misguidedly perhaps, but through thick and thin – seeing me whole.

At King's Cross in London a remorseful Michael strolled towards us from the ticket barrier, grinning and holding out a bunch of flowers. 'I want to go home,' Chrissie said, and the two of them got into a taxi Michael had waiting.

Eleven

I didn't see much of Chrissie and Michael after the Littleborough fiasco. I drifted out of their lives, and I drifted out of crime under no more conscious impulse than I'd drifted into it. For no reason life conspired to be nice. Blessings arrived all at once: a job, a girlfriend, a new and much better place to live. There was no great mystery to my straightening out. As Lucky Jim said, nice things are nicer than nasty ones.

From Chrissie I began to learn at least one important lesson. I glimpsed that we all spin, at different speeds, and each defiantly in our own trajectory; people are other, they are – like it or not – nothing but their defiant selves, and it wasn't in my power to become what Chrissie wanted because she defiantly didn't want anything of me. The seesaw of our interests rarely balanced. Whatever was going on, it became clear that I wasn't Hamlet, or a *cavaliere servente*, rushing up to help or save her like a knight. I was only the bit player, fit for a scene or two.

Five years later, when I was an editor at *Time Out*, one

of the typesetters came into the office dressed all in black. Her name was Miranda; she'd been at a funeral. 'Of no one you're likely to know,' she said. I knew that she thought I was very stuffy and ambitious, very straight. 'A lovely guy called Michael Granby.' I didn't hear what she said next. I walked back to my desk and stared out of the window. Our offices were five flights up. Down in the well of the building there was a mound of black rubbish sacks and a typewriter the star feature writer had tossed out during one of his tantrums. I thought of Michael then, billiard cue in hand, leaning down to smack the balls.

That might have been the end of the story. Aged twenty-two I'd been skidding and shifty, almost uncontrollably unsure. Yet somehow – a curious gift of my history – this had been hidden beneath a mask of composure. When at last I did start to make a living I tried never to think of that bad time, and if I did it was with a shudder of relief, grateful that I hadn't been caught. I'd been very, very lucky. I almost couldn't believe how lucky; it didn't seem right.

Some of the stuff from the robberies – Harry Johnston's Rolex, bits and bobs from the Robinsons' – was wrapped in newspaper and hidden away in boxes at the back of a cupboard in my flat, but I took care not to look. Only the stolen first editions were on proud display, mixed in with all those that I'd bought or been given. I could, and still can, remember where and how I got each one. I stopped suffering from migraine. It all came to seem like a dream.

I never told anyone, I was never even tempted. I couldn't

bear for anyone to guess at how messy and unformed I'd been. I'd been such a blank. Only theft had brought a beginning character of my own; I felt shame not because those acts were immoral or against the law but because they'd been expressions of a raw me which had to be suppressed at any cost. With writing came a second stab at independent identity and for years something cohered – nothing more than blend of work, place and love, until all of a sudden the planks loosened and I gained another look at the chaos beneath the keel.

This was in 1991. I'd finally finished and published one book, and was writing another, a novel, a re-imagining of my relationship with my father – my life as a book, which I knew would end with the father-character's death. Now the death of my own became material. I didn't ask his permission or show him any of the writing. The unspoken deal, my unspoken deal, was that so long as I didn't condemn him for what he'd done I was at liberty to play fast and loose with the facts of his life and mine. I always met him notebook in hand, even when he was in hospital, ready to shoot off to the gents and jot down anything juicy. I was stealing his past.

His confession came out bits at a time. He talked about the money he'd embezzled and blown: £1,500 on a fake passport; another £1,500 to be taken by small boat across to France; £3,000 more to get to South America. He talked about the long ago past in Bradford. Aged sixteen he had his first job, with a wool merchant in the Victorian heart of Bradford. I've a photo taken of him at this time, in a double-breasted suit with his hair slicked back like a little Jimmy Cagney. He worked standing, at a high desk in a room filled with the drowsy sweet smell of lanolin. He made a record of what came in an out of the warehouse, not only wool but camel hair and mink. Once he opened a crate from Shanghai; there were thousands of pig tails inside.

All these years he'd been back he'd promised me he'd been going straight. He'd sold houses. TV ads showed the head of the company – craggy faced, he'd been an actor – swooping about in a helicopter. You were no one unless you owned your own home. My father had his, two up, two down on an estate with hundreds of identical others. All the streets were named after American astronauts. He lived on Neil Armstrong Way.

Now he confessed that there was one last problem: he had several birth certificates, he'd applied for them through Somerset House the way the character did in Frederick Forsyth's *The Day of the Jackal* and he'd been using them to claim social security under assumed names; it was all going to go on unravelling after his death.

I grabbed at the chance. 'This has got to stop,' I said. 'Tell me where they are. Tell me where all your papers are. I'll take care of it now.'

'I'm not a kid,' he said with snappish sharpness.

That was it: another part of the deal, *my* deal, was that he had no right to question my wishes. Especially he was forbidden to lose his temper. I turned and walked out; I would happily have never seen him again.

I went back five or six days later.

'Dad the forger,' he said with a contrite smile.

I nearly told him the Flann O'Brien story. I'd often wondered if the bank manager and the friendly old rozzer on his Doc Marten soles had their own versions, recounted in the pub, or over a gin and tonic, of the Bomb Squad being called in to defuse *The Third Policeman* and a fraudster who had the nerve to ask for his briefcase back. It was a great story, just the kind of thing Dad liked.

I was educated, a literary man. I had a nice flat, nice clothes; I'd pegged myself into England in a way he hadn't managed, and both of us were proud of that. And there was something else: my father was a criminal who fancied himself a classy person; I'd been given the privilege of a classy education and had fancied myself a criminal. I knew something about myself he'd never dream, and was quite happy to feel smug and superior. He had an idea of me I didn't want to shatter. I didn't tell him.

The book was written in alternating states: exhilaration, rage. We were friends, we loved each other; yet so much was left unsaid. My anger came out only at odd moments. His illness made me realize how raw I still felt. I bathed him, I mopped up his mess; I gained his trust and bore my loot away.

My father didn't die. There was a remission, enabling him to move back north, to a small flat from which – suddenly, startlingly alive – he plotted junkets to cricket or the races. He even started to woo my mother again, until I put a stop to it. I was worried about my stepfather, and I didn't want reminding that I'd been the offspring of such a rapprochement. 'Cut it out, Dad, all right?'

He confessed that he'd joined the Freemasons again.

'Rudyard Kipling was very keen,' he said.

'But what do they do?'

'Oh, you know, ride the electric goat, that sort of thing,' he said, and strolled away, not David Niven perhaps, but a survivor, jaunty and chipper as Charlie Chaplin; I was struck by the wealth and sadness of a life lived so strenuously against the grain, and left to contemplate the mystery of the electric goat.

We spent a day at the cricket, and, after lunch, coming back from the refreshment tent, I had to search for him in the crowd. Beer in one hand, the other up on the seat beside him, wearing sunglasses and a pale summer jacket, he lifted his hand to wave.

'I'm Micawber,' he said. 'And you're my Charlie D.!'

I knew something darker was going on.

My father's grandfather had a farm in the north of England, not far from Newcastle. Shortly after the turn of the century he sold up and bought another, to the south, but not that far, in west Yorkshire; this seemed smart, because a thriving Bradford funeral business came along with the deal and Bradford was then one of the richest cities in Europe, thanks to a wool-manufacturing industry which prospered selling cloth for uniforms to both sides in the Franco-Prussian war of 1870–71. Bradford's vulgar wealth was well established; in *The Wasteland* T.S. Eliot wrote of 'the silk hat on a Bradford millionaire'.

My great-grandfather had three sons. The eldest inherited the farm, and the youngest was Uncle Billy who 'drank and he drank and he drank and he died at forty-four,' my mother said. The son in the middle was my grandfather, Bert Rayner, and he got the funeral business.

The son who inherited the farm added to his already considerable fortune and had three sons of his own. The youngest of these, Uncle Jimmy, was 'a lovable rogue', my mother said, 'a real rapscallion'. He certainly didn't suit the pattern required of a Yorkshire squire's son. He stole cars. He danced to American jazz and smoked marijuana, not easy to get hold of in provincial England in the 1950s. My father gave Uncle Jimmy a job when his own father kicked him off the farm, which meant that he was around a lot at our house. He ran errands for my mother, sneaked cigarettes to my sister, then aged eleven. He and I got on famously. When I let my brother's mice out of their cage in the kitchen and they seemed to be everywhere, a scratching flurry, it was to Uncle Jimmy that I turned.

'Jimmy,' I said. 'One's gone in the oven.'

Having retrieved the mouse, Uncle Jimmy looked at me with an odd pride. 'There was Uncle Billy, then there was me. And this one's next. Oh aye, Richard's next.'

Uncle Jimmy burned his father's barn.

My mother told me this only a few months ago. For years I thought I knew the story, which I'd heard from my father while he was sick. He told me that Uncle Billy had been the one who'd run away. I never heard anything from him about Uncle Jimmy, and therefore certainly not about the barn. What a detail! What anger or passion made him do it? My mother didn't know, and the barn – which had been full of hay – was completely destroyed. The sky was lit for miles around.

Soon afterwards Uncle Jimmy went somewhere, perhaps into the merchant navy, to Canada or America or Australia. No one knows. He was never heard of again. He vanished off the face of the earth.

There's the line in Balzac, about the one crime behind the making of every great fortune. My father believed there was but one injustice behind the undoing of his. He'd been cheated because though the Rayners had once owned two businesses it had been the duff funeral directorship that came down on his side. The fortune and the prosperous Harrogate farmlands went to his uncles and cousins. 'All that green,' he said. 'Green fields. Green shooting jackets. Green rubber boots they splash around in. Even the Range Rover is green.'

He never mentioned anything about Uncle Jimmy, who'd been on the green side of the family, who'd vanished without trace, who'd burned the barn so the sky was a beacon. He kept quiet about that, though he himself had made the kind of journey the Rayner men persuade themselves others only dream of, with all the detours and little trips on the side, away from their responsibilities and their own opinion of themselves. Perhaps this particular item of family history frightened him with its suggestion that things weren't decided by money and class after all, but character.

In my mother's and my father's telling of the story there were two details in common: someone had vanished, and that same someone had stood over me and predicted that I was the next delinquent in line. Grim Yorkshire humour, no doubt, but then again the story didn't go, 'He'll do yer well, that one,' or 'Look at the 'ead on 'im,' or even 'Ugly little beggar, ain't he?'

The general line was, *He's next.*

My book was duly finished. It is, of course, I told my father as I handed him a copy, a fiction. He never told me what he thought about it, and I never asked. A part of him would have been flattered, but he'd also have been left in no doubt that a job had been done. I'd been, for once, entirely clear about my intent. In all the hullaballoo I failed to give events their proper weight. I arranged the hullaballoo so I wouldn't have to.

I burned his barn.

I left England as arranged. I sold my flat and put all my books into storage, along with my long-hidden boxes of loot. I ended a five-year affair to join Paivi in Los Angeles. I orchestrated the smash-up with a recklessness that takes my breath away. I *fled* England, and I never heard from my father again.

Paivi grew up with her six brothers and sisters in Pyhajarvi, a small village in northern Finland. The village was approached down a narrow road through archways of birch and pine. In summer it was the greenest, bluest place in the world – nothing but trees, lake, and sky. In winter, when snow came for six months at a stretch, all colour was sucked back into white and grey. On Christmas Eve candles were placed on the graves of relatives, one candle per soul, and since in Pyhajarvi the dead far outnumbered the living, on that night the entire village was aglow, thousands of souls flickering in the frost. In the past, during winter dead bodies had been kept on an island all by themselves across the lake, because the frozen ground was too hard to dig a grave. These days a gravedigger went to work with dynamite, and since he was a drunk, the explosions were sometimes spectacular. March was a month of overwhelming greyness, the suicide month, and spring didn't come until late May, with a tiny yellow flower called widows' leaf and the rich smell of the earth as it started to thaw. Even then a sudden back winter might strike, and kill birds stone dead where they sang in the trees. August was the romantic time. After the weeks of midnight sun they saw the moon again. The moon looked slightly red and soft.

I knew from the first moment I saw her. I thought of Pasternak's lovely line: 'You took down my life from the shelf and blew the dust from my name.' I very much wanted the dust blown from my name.

Love at first sight – always a pipe-dream, a fantasy at which two parties take a colluding tilt – is sometimes a fantasy that turns out to be prescient, made real by events.

Our own love at first sight turned to something else, difficult but true. At night our bedroom in Hollywood filled with smells of jasmine and honeysuckle. Lying next to each other we heard gunshots, some rumble down on the neighbourhood crack alley. Helicopters passed fifty feet overheard, rude intrusions we felt first in our shaking chests and ribs, and we'd wake to find the room flooded with blue electric light – the LAPD had decided to take our picture. And yet it was the most beautiful room I'd ever slept in. The morning caught other effects, lozenges of sunlight moving the walls and ceilings, miracles that happened daily, thought out and stage managed over fifty years by Cecil B. DeMille, who'd copied the building brick for brick from one he'd seen in Spain. Once, at dawn, there was an earthquake; the walls shook and then wafted, my vision trembled and I was surprised by the noise, rattles and bangs that seemed not to come from the house but were as if made by the tremor itself. Paivi got up and stood under the door, like you're supposed to, while I was still too sleepy to bother. For a rapt moment there were no screams or sirens or car alarms; the city held its breath, there was only the sound of water in the fountain in the courtyard, slapping from side to side.

We went to a party, high up above the city on Mulholland Drive. With darkness came a sudden chill. Fog rose layer after layer from the floors of the canyons. The men stood around making jokes. 'Hey, "Industrial Light and Magic". Did Spielberg fix this?' Fog kept coming. It grew cold and we had to wrap ourselves in sweaters and blankets. Someone brought lamps from inside the house, and these were lit along with torches set at the end of bamboo sticks. The fog was of such density that it reflected back the flickering lights. Dense glowing bulbs were made by the moisture around each lamp and torch. The fog reached all the way up to the house and then stopped. Only wisps strayed above. Los Angeles was invisible below. It might not have been there, it might have sunk and disappeared for all we knew. The deck was floating on fog like a ship.

When condensation formed on my eyelashes, making rainbows, I was swept back fifteen years to Cambridge, with the college bells arguing the hour as I walked back through the cloisters of Emmanuel College to my rooms and my dreams. As Paivi and I drove away, down into the fog and Coldwater Canyon, a car came towards us with its uprushing headlights gauzy and contorted out of all proportion. Then it too was gone and fog settled back around, a chrysalis, touching everything with silence and solitude.

I was asleep that night when the phone rang. My sister didn't have to tell me, I knew. My father had died. He'd had a heart attack and she'd found him in the bathroom, dressed in his pyjamas, toothbrush in hand with the toothpaste still on it. There wasn't even a dab on the floor.

I'd been out of England a little more than two weeks. I came to fear, to be certain, that I'd killed him with my book.

*

The funeral was held outside York. The crematorium was a squat building of red brick and the priest was coloured to match, left too long in the sun. He had a harsh Northern Irish accent and took the service at a sprint, with punishment in mind, pausing only to mention that 'the dead one' hadn't been much of a Catholic, and that 'he had lived life to the full', phrases made ripe with condemnation and the hint that the dead one would find his current state as hectic as life itself, but in a warmer venue.

We tried to laugh it off. My father had himself enjoyed death's melodrama and farce – he used to talk about his own adventures in the business. Wood had been scarce at the end of WWII. Coffins had been made from orange boxes. Once, when he'd been a bearer, he'd slipped at the end of the service coming down the church steps. The corpse slid down the coffin like a sack of potatoes and its feet popped out the end. 'The legs hung there like the sad half of a ventriloquist's dummy,' he'd said.

There were aspects of his own death he might have appreciated – not just the priest, but the misspelling of his name on the coffin: John Bertram Ray*nor*. He was cremated as he'd spent so much of his life – with a name not exactly his own. Even his death was shifty. One of the undertakers made an unexpected entrance at the hotel where we all went for something to eat afterwards. He came in still wearing black top hat and sponge-bag trousers. Red in the face, and with a tufty ginger moustache, on seeing us he made great ceremony of raising his hat. Then he put it back on again and gulped at a pint of Guinness. Creamy froth thickened the moustache.

I tried to talk to everyone who was there. So few people: my brother, my sister, and their partners; my mother and my stepfather, very shaky himself; my nephews and their girlfriends. There was one friend of his, a spry old fellow with a silver RAF button in his lapel. 'I read about it in the paper,' he said. 'I'm afraid I hadn't seen him in over thirty years.'

I was surprised and annoyed when friends in Los Angeles told me how beaten I looked, or how bad I sounded on the phone. I really didn't feel too terrible. I didn't think so. Then one morning I held the edge of the bathroom door with my left hand, swung it back and then quickly towards me again while ducking my head forward as hard as I could. *Bang.* I did it again. *Bang.* Pause. *Bang.*

I floated above most of the rest of the day, after which I discovered the kitchen table would do as well. *Bang. Bang.* There was a lump on my forehead with a little cut in it, a smitten golf ball. That night, as we passed through the underpass on Franklin Avenue, we stopped for a red light. Traffic swished north and south on the Hollywood freeway above. On the wall of the underpass there was a mural, in Day-Glo pink, yellow and black, of a man whose skull was unreeling like a reel of computer tape. Suddenly I had my hands clamped to the back of my neck. My elbows were stuck out like wings. Something made an extraordinary noise, and it was me; I howled.

I didn't feel I was fighting a battle. I smashed doors, mugs, and plates. I smashed the phone when it told me things I didn't wish to hear. At dinner I smashed a glass candlestick with the candle still burning – hot wax splashed on the floor, and into our food. It dripped down the wall and, cooling, made stalactites off the edge of the table.

Paivi found herself face to face with a stranger. 'These episodes come out of nowhere,' she said. 'Like lightning out of a clear sky.' I felt like the thing the sky had trodden on, shattered. I couldn't work, it made me just dizzy. I was falling.

I took refuge in books. I read books as usual, but faster, more. I bought them by the dozen and soon filled the shelves in our apartment so I had to pile them on the floor. I haunted used book stores all over Los Angeles. There was one on the Westside, owned and run by Barnaby, a slender Jew always dressed in black. In general he came on like Hamlet – older and more grizzled, but still ticking off Ophelia. If an unknowing customer came in off the street and asked for, say, Danielle Steele (and why not?) Barnaby let rip with a laugh of brutal scorn. His prices were also by way of literary judgement. Barnaby was, for instance, a big Bertrand Russell fan, and in the philosophy section he had a nice set of the Little, Brown/Atlantic edition of the autobiography, but at $25 a volume. Quite ridiculous! For such cases I travelled with a selection of Dixon Ticonderoga pencils, the ones with the erasers on the end, and engaged in a spot of re-reviewing. That's to say I rubbed out Barnaby's price and substituted my own ball-park notion.

'I do his hand very well, though I do say so myself,' I told Paivi, expecting her to be amused.

'Oh,' she said, again. 'That's wrong. You're cheating him.'

My whole character became porous.

No, no, I explained, I didn't buy the books myself but left them for other customers to make happy discoveries. Once I was in there when I saw a fellow come upon a first edition by Marguerite Duras that I'd independently re-assessed. He danced a funny little jig of triumph, like Hitler accepting the surrender of France in the railway carriage at Compiègne.

'Another book case,' I said.

'My mystery man,' Paivi said, nonchalance more effective than attack. 'My pencil-wielding bandit, packing lead.'

When we took to the road I bought Mona Wilson's biography of Blake, the old Hart-Davis edition, from a store at the end of the Bay Bridge in San Francisco, and, on the way out, I stole an unusual edition of Nathanael West's *Miss Lonelyhearts*, from the 1960s, an Avon paperback, shaped like an actual heart, a broken heart. With that same thrill and tingle I opened my jacket, closed it quickly, and walked out to the car half-sunk in a trance, *Miss Lonelyhearts* curved around my ribs, the first book I'd stolen in fifteen years. The price inside the cracked heart of a cover was $1.95. 'You must be absolutely out of your mind,' I said to myself, 'you're not this person any more.' Obviously I still was that person. One day, browsing at a store up in Glendale, I opened a book and my eye fell on the word 'migraine'. The green carpet beneath my feet started to leap and shimmer. Moments later I was in the haze. Minutes after that I collapsed in the back of the car.

Then it was the Los Angeles riots, terrible public events which came to an absurdly personal point when, as we watched two people not so unlike ourselves stuff their Volvo with looted booty, I expressed my self-righteous outrage – they couldn't conceivably need this stuff, and Paivi made with the eyebrow music and said: 'Yes, Richard. But what if the store were filled with Nabokov first editions?'

A core of my life had been secrecy. I'd kept quiet about my parents' divorce and about my father's disappearance. I'd lied about where I lived when I was at school and where I went to school when I was at home, whichever home it was, and there'd been a few. I lied at Cambridge and in London, and then it turned out I really was like the Spartan boy in the story, maiming myself with the hidden.

Now I'd dismantled and smashed the persona that I'd spent nearly fifteen years carving out. As reckless gestures go, it was a dilly, and I did it with glee. It nearly took me under: to my surprise, I found myself spinning, much as I had in my early twenties. I didn't understand how this could be happening. Life, work – they were connected, of course, but not necessarily by a fault line.

I'd told no one all those years about my cheque-book spree, the housebreaking, the adventure with Chrissie and Michael. So I told Paivi more and more, things I thought I'd never reveal to anyone. Such as: at Cambridge I once slept with a man, a theology don with curly hair and dark good looks. The experience made me gather what I'd assumed all along, that I'd prefer sex with women; but, since I'd also assumed sexual identity to be a mask like any other, and that everyone is a mixture of inclinations, I'd thought I should give it a try at least once.

'What was it like?' asked Paivi.

'Fine,' I said. 'Not especially religious.'

She was unfazed, but the clock stopped when I confessed about David and Mary, the non-existent siblings I'd invented when I first met her. I'd wanted her sympathy. I'd felt the warmth and energy she'd gained from growing up with all those brothers and sisters and at that moment I'd wished a big family for myself. As time had gone on, and I'd got to know her better and better, often telling her stories about Helen and Keith, my real brother and sister, I'd tried to keep quiet about the fictional other two. There were no fascinating reports from Lompoc or Bali, no niggly little problems about where the kids should be sent to school. They were mysterious, unreal, except in this one regard – their ghostly presence was a reminder that I could flip back into my old floppy self. What did it matter who I was, when I could be someone different so easily?

I knew I had to tell her. The idea gave me goosebumps. When at last I did it happened by mistake, a wished-for and meant mistake. 'I remember when the three of us were kids,' I said. *The three of us*: as far as Paivi knew there were five. I confessed. I took her hand and held it tight. 'David and Mary don't exist,' I said. 'I made them up.'

She thumped me.

While it feels half nuts to admit that I told all this so I could get over the hump of confessing one last lie, there's a lot of truth in it as well. The instinct that life is good was where I began. The realization that my own life was cracked admitted the possibility that I'd fallen, that grace had to be asked for. In asking for it from her, I've pieced myself together.

My father never tried to shape me in his own image. I fear that it's happened anyway, though the only thing he ever actively taught me was how to tie a half-windsor knot. This was before I went away to the school in Wales, when he woke me in the middle of the night, made me dress and practise tying the knot until I'd got it right, then went away and shut the door, so that a cheese-slice wedge of light from the hallway disappeared soundlessly with him. I sometimes do still think that I killed him. I'm still in love with books, with writing, though the bright colours of that dream are chastened.

When a few weeks ago I thought I'd better tell my mother all about her son the thief and housebreaker there was a nervous little laugh before she said: 'You did all that? *Damn you.*' I asked her if she'd mind very much not saying that, though I'd begged for it, I suppose, the maternal stamp on my fondly nursed changeling status. The past is dangerous; handle it as though it was red hot. Calming down, she let go a long sigh, as of air let out of a cushion. 'You really did those things? *Oooooph*. You little sod.' My mother.

Paivi and I aren't in Hollywood these days. We're down by the beach, where the fog has taken longer than usual to rise this morning and, now, after midday, the smoke of my breath still adds to it. In the office where I work a spider stands balanced on the wall, while outside the palm trees are swaying to the gentlest of breezes, swaying almost as if beneath the mere weight of their own fronds. The gate at the front gives way with a welcome click. Paivi's home.

I veer between guilt at burdening her with all this and an exhilarated sense of renewal. I've described a sentimental education, the me that was 'me' when I first felt that, and it's been a more obvious and bold statement than I thought I'd ever dare, so much childish hope and fear crystallized, part of an attempt to set a bent course straight.

I went diving once, falling backwards off the boat into clear warm water and down towards the sunken remains of a city, destroyed by an earthquake some three thousand years ago. There was a labyrinth of wrecked columns, and there were archways and huge stone blocks, planted in sand now, but mapping out streets, squares, the semicircle of an amphitheatre. I saw the after images of a used-up past, and also that which was present – haunting, aglow – real beyond the quarter-inch glass of the face mask.

I'm having to wring the thief out of me drop by drop.

Richard Rayner

The other day I was asked if I'd ever read John Stuart Mill's *Autobiography*, the philosopher's story of his own odd coming of age; well, yes, I blurted out, I once stole a first edition.